God Lives
in
Stoke-On-Trent

Valerie Simm Turner

PENTALPHA
PUBLISHING
EDINBURGH
☆

God Lives in Stoke on Trent
© *Valerie Simm Turner 2020*
Published by Pentalpha Publishing Edinburgh

Cover design: MadCow
All enquiries to pentalphapublishing@live.co.uk
First published by Pentalpha Publishing Edinburgh
2020.

ISBN: 9798692958310

Dedicated to
Bhagavan Shri Satya Sai Baba
my Beloved Teacher

CHAPTER ONE

In every human being Divinity is present in a subtle form. But man is deluded by this unmanifested presence of the Divine into believing that God does not exist. The innumerable waves on the vast ocean contain the same water as the ocean regardless of their forms. Likewise, although human beings have myriads of names and forms, each is a wave on the ocean of Sath-Chith-Ananda *(Being-Awareness-Bliss).*

- Sathya Sai Baba

'JESUS WANTS ME FOR A SUNBEAM.'

As I sang this in the Methodist Church in Hanley, Stoke-on-Trent, a scrawny child of seven, I truly believed it was so. I also believed in Santa Claus, until I 'found' all my presents hidden at the back of the wardrobe in my parents' bedroom. As I look back on the wardrobe scaling incident, I am amazed at the agility I had.

The wardrobe was placed at an angle in the corner of the room expressly to foil any attempt on my part at getting at my presents. This would be akin to my climbing a sheer cliff face of at least fifteen feet now. How I got back again is yet another testimony to my determination to achieve my goals.

I can still remember the absolute let down of that Christmas morning when I had to pretend to be surprised as I opened parcel after parcel of goodies already fingered. To this day I prefer to leave my presents wrapped for as long as I can and thoroughly enjoy the suspense before I open them. I suppose the realisation that grown-ups tell such whopping lies about such important events as the one involving the benevolent gift giver Santa prepared me to question all things that grown-ups said.

All my life I have questioned everything.

My dearest friend once said of me that if a fly walked across the window I would want to know why. I used to scold myself for this questioning of everything, seeing it as a definite disadvantage when I started on my spiritual path, and tried to accept things which were completely foreign and which appeared very strange to the world as I knew it. I gave up this criticism of myself when I realised the importance of discrimination - what William Bloom describes as wearing our 'bull-shit' antenna. There really are poor crazy people out there and when sailing on such uncharted seas it is no surprise that there are great devotees on 'Fantasy Island'.

The event which put the final piece of the jigsaw into my already suspicious notion that the whole Jesus stuff was also made up, was the death at fifty-eight of my beloved Grandmother. Mama had reared me from my birth when I lived in the same house with her and my mother and my mother's four sisters. I can remember being confused when I was told that my real mother was the beautiful eldest daughter. Mum was twenty-two when she had me, and dad just eighteen. They were married in July and I was born in November, which was shocking for the times, although there was a war raging so I think the scandal would soon be forgotten.

My grandmother was the wisest woman I had ever known. In contrast to her rather frivolous daughters she had a palpable inner calm and wisdom. When the neighbours in our street had a problem they couldn't solve themselves, then Mama would be sent for. She used to lay out the dead people for the undertaker and tend to any sick child. In fact my Uncle, her son, told me that as at the time doctors had to be paid by the patient and the area being poor, the good Doctor of the local area gave her bandages and simple medicines so that she could minister to the very poor who could not afford to pay to see him. This may explain the only book in the house which was always on her stairs, out of the way of my prying eyes which nevertheless I loved to creep up the stairs to look at. This book was like nothing I had seen before. It had figures of males and females and when the top layer of skin was removed, showed the blood vessels and muscles and with layer after layer all the, to me, shocking details of the human body were arrayed. The part of the book which scared and fascinated me the most though was the graphic full colour lurid illustrations of various skin diseases.

She was stoic in the way she coped with a difficult life: her husband and soulmate had died at thirty-eight leaving her with six children, the eldest sixteen and the youngest two. She had contracted silicosis from the tile factory she worked in and this triggered T.B. I loved her so much and enjoyed tearing newspaper into small squares for her to spit into and throw into the fire - this before the days of expensive paper handkerchiefs.

On the day she died in a sanatorium, I walked with my mother the five miles to my father's workplace to tell him. We must have looked a comical pair, clutching each other's hands and wailing as we walked. My mother was muttering between her sobs, 'There is no God. How can there be to let a good woman like my mother suffer so much?'

That was good enough for me. At the age of thirteen I threw out the whole spiritual package and decided that just as I could live without Santa Claus then I could also live without God.

CHAPTER TWO

In western countries now, God is denied, and man is relying on himself. He exaggerates his own intelligence and sense of adventure and prides himself on the advance he has made through science and technology. But, intelligence without equanimity is filling mental hospitals. Peace is fleeing from the hearts of men and women: social harmony is becoming a distant dream; international concord is a mirage pursued by a few. Man travels to the moon, but does not explore his own inner levels of consciousness, and understanding them, cleanse them and control them.

- Sathya Sai Baba

A CURTAIN WAS DRAWN OVER the spiritual side of my life and I threw myself into the whole deal of job, dating and marriage.

The birth of my son after two years of marriage was the highlight of my life and I fell in love with him as the nurse gave him to me after a very easy birth. He had a perfectly shaped head for birthing - his dad called him 'bullet head'.

I had always intended to have three children so it was again with great joy when my second baby was on the way three years later. Before the birth of my second child I truly believed I was made for childbirth, my son's birth had been so easy and I could see no reason why this birth should not follow a similar pattern. I was wrong. To begin with, the doctor who correctly forecasted the time of arrival of my son had given a date for this birth of one month later than the midwives at the clinic. The midwives insisted on my preparing for the earlier date as I was having this one at home and had to have the birthing room with my home kit all ready.

Any mother will know what the last month of pregnancy is like: it seems as though time has telescoped out and one month seems like six. Of course, the doctor was spot on, but by the time our baby arrived I felt I had had a very prolonged pregnancy. Our beautiful 8 lbs daughter made up for lost time when she did decide to grace us with her presence.

I started with my first contraction at ten o'clock and she was born at four minutes past one on Sunday morning. Because I am small framed – 5ft 2ins - and she a largish baby I really struggled to give birth. The midwife - a great farmer's wife type who clumped up the stairs in heavy boots - grew a little alarmed during the birth and called to my husband to help her. He was just about to slide down the bedroom door, his face ashen - as much from running up and down stairs having to fetch staggering amounts of water, etc., for her as from his fright at what was happening. I never know to this day what she did with all the water.

From my side of the drama I reached a point where I couldn't push the baby out and yet when I stopped pushing she didn't slip back to give me the temporary reprieve between contractions, and it felt as though she was stuck in my pelvic bone. The pain was so intense - and I had no relief from drugs as my labour had been too quick for any injection and one whiff of the gas and air machine made me violently sick all over the floor. I screamed and had the sensation of whooshing along a dark tunnel and I 'knew' that I was dying.

At the end of this tunnel was a light which I also knew was God. The absolutely incredible feeling of love which filled me from this light source was so intense that I longed with heart and soul to go to Him. I then remembered that I was giving birth and that the baby would have no mother, so the next instant I was back in the room feeling the excruciating pain and with the midwife and my husband yelling at me to push.

My husband afterwards said that I had not screamed I had simply lain very still and quiet and he and the midwife were unaware of the drama in front of their eyes. I could tell by the strange way he looked at me when I later told him what had happened that he thought I was deluded and I made a mental note not to tell anyone else.

As soon as the placenta was out - again this was very painful and the midwife was concerned that this was another baby - I heard the most wonderful celebratory peal of bells from St Werburgh, a local church a matter of half a mile away. I remarked to my husband that I thought it was a wonderful omen that they were pealing the bells on the day our daughter was born and of course it was Sunday. It was his puzzled look that made me realise this was one a.m! I truly heard the bells with my external listening device and not my inner; in fact, I didn't know I had an inner at the time.

From this point on I started to shake and my teeth were chattering so much it sounded like someone playing the spoons. The midwife piled blanket upon blanket on me and I expect she thought I was suffering from shock. I had the strange sensation of pins and needles which developed into numbness which slowly spread from my toes and fingers into my arms and legs like a creeping paralysis. I was, however, undisturbed and lay in a blissful state.

It was not until nearly eighteen years later that I experienced this strange sensation again when I was engaged in a connected breath technique called 'Rebirthing'.

Although I didn't tell anyone else about this experience it had a profound effect on my spirituality. I now knew God and didn't need to believe anything. He/she/it just is, and I now knew this. I also knew that we don't die. I didn't ever have the sensation that I had left my body behind, in fact I felt whole and essentially me, but with much greater capabilities such as the feeling that I was 'whooshing' down the tunnel rather than walking or running. I suppose it would be the nearest to how I imagine it's like to fly.

CHAPTER THREE

The one who is immersed in body consciousness is a prey to all kinds of troubles and worries. It should be realised that the body is only an instrument and is bound to perish some time or other. When death is bound to follow birth, why worry about it?

God is not separate from you. Strive to strengthen this sense of oneness with the Divine. This was the way Mira experienced the presence of Krishna in her heart when her husband, the Maharana, expelled her from the Krishna temple built by him.

- Sathya Sai Baba

TO ALL OUTER APPEARANCES I was the normal Val - well as normal as I've ever been - but inside I was changed.

I felt a need to search for God in the church which was where I expected Him to be so I went to St Werburgh and sat with the congregation and prayed and prayed:

'Please, God, will you show yourself to me if you are here in this church?' Nothing.

I went about three times and still nothing. The rest of the congregation seemed rather old and I suspected that the social aspect was the reason most of them were there - or perhaps I'm not being fair to them. At least to me at the time it seemed like this. I was also very dismayed at the bitterness and what I thought lack of love expressed by some of the people there.

At this time I was arranging for our daughter's christening. Our son had been christened at the church where we were married but this was near my parents' home and vicars were not very pleased to christen out of their parish. Again, St Werburgh was the obvious choice, and the vicar insisted on instruction for godparents and parents as we were not among his flock.

This coincided wonderfully with my search for God because I had the chance to talk at length to one of 'them'. He was a young curate and I think he enjoyed our chats over coffee in my kitchen. At least he said he paid more visits than he usually did in such cases. I talked of my search for God - not my experience at the birth - and at the end of his visits he said that he thought there were two kinds of people (only two!) one was what he called a 'God person' and the other a 'people's person' and he decided that I was the latter. He said he thought I obviously cared for people and helped the needy (I had told him of my work for Oxfam) and yet I would never experience God. What conceit, and yet he meant it kindly and was operating within the limits of his knowledge and experience at that time.

Something faint and distant must have echoed in my brain because I suddenly remembered my

Sunday School days at the Methodist Chapel and I thought I'd look to see if God was in the chapel.

We had at the time a small chapel about a quarter of a mile from St Werburgh and, as befits the Methodist doctrine, this was much smaller and plainer than the church. I sat at the back and listened on two Sundays while the lay preacher who provided the sermon screamed hell fire and damnation at us for being the sinners that he said we were.

I knew this was not God - not the God I had experienced during the near-death experience at the birth. My experience of God was of love not fear.

On the second Sunday I was sitting at the back as usual and I said to God, 'This is the last time I will come to search for you and maybe you can only be reached when we die (or nearly die, as I had), and not in life ' Almost as soon as the words were out I saw a bolt of light enter through a long plain glass window at the back of the chapel which hit me straight in the heart. Talk about thunderbolts! I was shaken rigid and tears started to flow from my eyes. I remember being amused that when I'd heard of and read of people 'seeing the light'. I thought they meant that they had clearer understanding yet in fact they meant an actual light.

The lay preacher was still thumping the lectern and projecting his own inner anger and fear onto us in the guise of speaking about God and I just had to get out of there without anyone seeing my streaming eyes.

The usual format in churches as well as chapels is for the priest to stand by the door and shake hands with the congregation as they leave. It is also usual that the congregation gather in groups for a little chat before leaving. There was no way I could take part in this ritual with tears still streaming down my face and how could I tell anyone what had happened?

I shot like a frightened rabbit out through the door as the preacher was just threading his way through the pews and I hit the fresh air with a sigh of relief

The sky was completely clouded over and a fine drizzle dampened the air, so no actual sunlight could be responsible for the bolt of light hitting me through the window minutes before.

I raced home tears still streaming down my face. When I reached the house, I burst in upon my husband who had been minding the children, and cried out to him, 'God is Love, God is Joy.' I then went on to share with this bemused man what had happened and to explain my new knowledge that God was not the stern, fearful and ultra-serious God as depicted by the church but was a living, joyful and real God who communicated with ordinary mortals like me and that he loves each and every one of us just as we are.

I had one last revelation before I settled down to rear my children and get on with the more earthbound side of my life, albeit with a different attitude to that previously held.

I was peeling potatoes for dinner by the kitchen window when, without any prompting on my part, God again let me feel his active presence. A wave of joy and love hit me and again I started to cry. I then 'knew' that I didn't necessarily have to go to church to find Him, He was also 'outside' in everyday life.

CHAPTER FOUR

The age span 16-30 is crucial, for that is the period when life adds sweetness to itself, when talents, skills, and attitudes are accumulated, sublimated, and sanctified. If the tonic of unselfish service is administered to the mind during this period, life's mission is fulfilled - for the process of sublimation and sanctification will be hastened by this tonic. Do not serve for the sake of reward, attracting attention, or earning gratitude, or from a sense of pride at your own superiority in skill, wealth, status, or authority. Serve because you are urged by Love. When you succeed, ascribe the success to the Grace of God who urged you on, as Love within you. When you fail, ascribe the failure to your own inadequacy, insincerity, or ignorance.

- Sathya Sai Baba

LOOKING BACK NOW, I can see that I became more compassionate although I had always been a compassionate child. I remember being very upset when another child was singled out and bullied. This, perhaps, is a little surprising as I was not myself bullied. I was a popular, gregarious child who could hold her own in any fight.

My love of my fellows, however, did increase and I also spontaneously said a prayer without fail every night asking God not only to care for my family but also that He would help those in need, whatever their need. I remember praying for those children who were being abused after a particular horrific event reported in the news at the time, and then I also had a sudden thought that the abusers were also in need of God's help, so I added to my nightly prayer: 'God please help the abused and also their abusers.'

I certainly didn't lead an abstemious life after my near-death experience. I had always wanted to try things out for myself, never accepting that the fire burns until I had stuck my finger in to see. My mother told me that if I was told that something was dangerous it was a sure sign I would do that very thing. I can remember as a child feeling very proud when the big boys let me join them in their game of 'duffers' which involved highly dangerous climbing over rusting cars and obsolete war tanks and machinery in a scrap yard near to my parents' house. I was beside myself with pride and joy when they said I was braver and more agile than some of the older boys. More stupid, perhaps, as I went crying home from one such foray into the yard with a badly bitten tongue after I had jumped off the twenty-foot roof of a building under construction. I made a perfect landing onto a pile of sand, but unfortunately my knee came up before it should to hit my chin which caught the tongue I must have had sticking out in concentration.

I think the above gives a brief idea of the sort of child I was and the sort of adult I grew into.

I had to try everything for myself which included a brief taste of the soft drug scene. I also had a rather varied range of jobs.

I was secretary to an accountant from 9am - 5.30pm and then in order to augment my pittance of pay I went up the road to work from 6pm -10pm as a cinema usherette. What I saw on the back row from the gallery was an eye opener to me at sixteen.

I have also worked in rather dubious bars, as working in bars was a good way to earn money without affecting my role as a mother, an important and extremely enjoyable role to me. I wanted to be with the children during the day, so after my husband was fed and the children in bed, I would don my glad rags and hop down to the pub.

I once did an unofficial census of the barmaids I worked with at a local dance hall; there were about fourteen of them and nearly all were mothers who doted on their children and were very family orientated - not a bit like the usual male fantasy of the barmaid.

We dance hall bar staff also had our off duty fun time too, and about once a month we all piled into a coach to be driven to a sister night club which opened on the night ours was closed. This was the night we let our hair down and had lots of fun and lots of booze.

How easy it is to see a picture from a distance, and yet with nose pressed up to the glass only a splurge of colour is discernible. I can now look back and see that everything that happened to me was a preparation, a course at the university of life, and a necessary clearing house of past debts which was a preparation for my meeting God in human form.

Looking back, I can see that I had thrown myself into living a full life yet with something intangible missing. A feeling would catch me unawares every now and then that there must be something more to life than the usual way of living and that there had to be some purpose. This feeling was very fleeting, though, and very infrequent, and my life was so full that I think I would have gone on in this way if it hadn't been for the event which shattered my life.

CHAPTER FIVE

The existence of opposing qualities if part of the nature of life. For instance, pleasure and pain go together. Pain is often the means by which God tests human beings. They should welcome such tests, because they serve to promote one's spiritual development. You should welcome such tests and difficulties. By overcoming them your divinity is revealed. The Pandavas realised their Divinity only when they faced many ordeals during their exile.

- Sathya Sai Baba

MY DARLING SON HAD BEEN born on the 5th November at the Haywood Hospital, alias Colditz, a mere quarter of a mile from my home. On the same day a woman unknown to me also gave birth, and also to a son.

I remember the first time I met her it was outside the communal bathroom, the only one shared by about twenty rooms and so much in demand. I timidly walked to the door, timid because of the fear instilled in me by a particularly gruesome staff nurse and also at my most vulnerable with my first child. As I approached the bathroom door a woman waiting there turned to me and snapped,

'You'll have to wait, there's already somebody in there.' I thought this was not only stating the obvious, as she wouldn't have been waiting there if it was empty, and was also very rudely delivered 'I don't like her,' I thought, deciding to keep my distance.

For thirteen years from this time we were truly soul sisters. One day, after leaving hospital, as I was proudly wheeling my peaceful son accompanied by my mother on a shopping trip, I bumped into a wild woman with red bloodshot eyes and a rather dishevelled appearance. It was Beryl, the woman from outside the maternity bathroom.

I could hardly recognise her and we were forced to make at least a polite exchange. I asked her how she and the baby were and as she poured out her story my heart went out to her.

The baby did not sleep. She had to wheel him up and down in his pram in the living room of her house in order to stop him screaming so that her husband could sleep a little and be fit for work the next day. When her husband had gone to work, she took the baby to her mother who again wheeled him up and down while my friend had a little doze in her mother's bed. They lived like this for six months.

Our friendship deepened the more we saw of each other, and we saw a lot of each other. She could drive and had the use of her husband's car and we used to pile the babies in the back and set out to various beauty spots. Later, when I learned to drive - she was a wonderful additional driving instructor - and I had my daughter, the five of us would set out and visit country parks, wild life sanctuaries, goose fairs and many other exciting places.

The children loved it, and while they ran around my friend and I could have a good natter. And how we talked. We both had the same wicked sense of humour and we weren't together for five minutes before we would be in fits of laughter. I remember one evening excursion, without the children this time, when we visited a local spiritualist church and a rather batty old dear was issuing forth and was obviously enjoying the attention. She was in touch with various entities - or so she said - and had a very broad Stoke accent which she obviously felt was not in keeping with her exalted position, so she 'poshed' it up by sounding her aitches - in every place except where they should have been.

We had to leave the church because we didn't want to disrupt the meeting and outside in the deserted street Beryl wet her knickers she laughed so much. She had to take them off in the toilet of a nearby pub which we occasionally frequented.

We also worked together in a dance hall. She had never worked in a bar before so her job was glass washing, which paid less than serving in the bars. I can hear her laugh now, as she clanged glasses on each of the twelve bars to replenish stocks. I also remember her determination to become a barmaid.

In order to do this, she had to demonstrate an ability to remember the price of each drink and be extremely efficient at adding a sometimes long drinks list in her head. No computerised tills for us. We used to go swimming with the children and I remember us swimming side by side while I tested her bar abilities. We got some strange looks from our fellow swimmers as they saw the odd women swimming together and one shouting above the noise of the baths, 'Gin and tonic!' and the other shouting back 'three and eleven' This was before decimalisation.

She, too, was a compassionate person and as part of our desire to help those less fortunate we did voluntary 'Meals on Wheels'. I loved it. She drove and we both took meals to the old and sometimes disabled people. What a pair - I think we brought a little sunshine into a few sad lives as we laughed our way on our round. Since she had her less favourite people, I would take in their meals and she took in the few I had trouble with.

I remember one day, as we were threequarters of the way through our round, we dropped a tray of meals which the local dogs, ever alert, quickly gobbled up. We couldn't keep the old dears waiting while we drove back to the kitchen as most of them waited anxiously for what was sometimes their only visit, so, ever resourceful we nipped into the local chippy's and gave our customers a rare treat of fish and chips.

For weeks afterwards some of them asked when they were going to have them again as they had enjoyed them so much.

She was sent to me by God to be a source of support and love, and the joy of life we shared was a rare and beautiful thing. My husband, who worked at British Telecom, rather crudely said of her that she would laugh if her 'arse was on fire', and he jokingly offered to put a direct telephone line from her house to mine to save us the bother of dialling; this because we rang each other so often.

The warning bell heralding the end of the idyll came when she met me one day as I arrived at her house and asked me to feel her breast. I thought at first she was about to launch into a funny story about someone having their breast felt when I saw from her face that she was serious. I did feel, and yes there was a tiny hard lump about the size of a pea. I was as alarmed as she was herself and while I was there she made an appointment with the doctor for the following day.

The next day I also had an appointment with a psychologist who was giving me a battery of intelligence and aptitude tests as I was thinking of continuing my education now the children were growing up. On the morning in question I woke with a raging temperature and chronic sore throat and knew that I had started with 'flu'. I somehow took the tests, by this time with a splitting headache, and with my mind on my friend and her doctor's appointment. As soon as I finished the tests I drove to her house and as I entered the kitchen she was ironing with a great beaming face. She said the doctor had diagnosed a small cyst which he said was nothing to worry about. I was alarmed. I had read the publicity urging women to report any lump immediately and I didn't see how the doctor could be sure without at least a test of some kind.

I did voice my concern but did not argue as strongly as I felt because I did not want to dampen her euphoria and also because I felt as though I was dying. I spent the next few days unable to get out of bed and then developed bronchitis which lasted its customary two weeks,

Pointless as it is to look back and say 'if only', nevertheless I spent a lot of time distraught at not following my intuition and pushing more strongly for her to challenge the doctor's diagnosis.

The small lump grew from the size of a small pea to the size of a peach stone before we talked of lumps again. This time she was alerted and told the doctor she wanted to see a specialist. The dreadful day was not long in coming and I knew the worst when I arrived home one day to find her standing by her car in my driveway, a look of horror on her face. We didn't say a word but just clung together and wept on each other's shoulders.

I held her hand while they wheeled the trolley to the operating doors where the attendant sent me back to wait until she returned. She had caused a rumpus before this by refusing to sign the consent form giving the surgeon permission to slice off her breast if he felt it necessary. This was in the days when the solution to any breast problem was 'off with the breast', and she said she'd rather be dead than live with only one breast. Even though I didn't share this view, I would defend to the death anyone's right to decide what happens to her body, and, in fact I did vigorously defend her decision when others questioned me about it.

The lump was a malignant cancer and this was removed and a silicone prostheses inserted.

True to form, she took this in her stride and not only made a very quick recovery but laughed hilariously at her new very firm breast which stayed upright while the other flattened when she lay on her back while engaging in our favourite occupation - sunbathing. I remember we once went to a night-club with our husbands and as they were not very fond of dancing, they sat at our table talking cars or such like while the two of us danced together. Two unattached males, ever alert for the chance to grab females, didn't realise we already had our guardians and joined us on the dance floor. When the dance ended and we beat a hasty retreat before trouble with spouses brewed, Beryl was doubled up with laughter as she related to me the look of shock on her dance partner's face as his arm ' accidentally' brushed against her rock hard breast while he was dancing close to her.

I really did believe she would be one of the lucky ones and live a long, healthy life; she certainly had a positive approach and we continued in much the same way as we had before, except perhaps with even more appreciation of our friendship and life itself.

She was planning a birthday party to celebrate reaching her fortieth birthday on New Year's Eve and we spent uproarious times beforehand planning the games she was going to play. Not a simple drinks party for her - she had used her abundant creativity and joy of life to invent some crazy games and true to form she had the props all ready a few months before the great day. This was going to be the party to end all parties.

All appeared well until one day in early December I was in her kitchen drinking coffee when she started to cry.

She told me she had been feeling very sick and knew that the cancer had returned. She had made an appointment with the doctor and had decided to see if she could go for a new test - an examination on something called a scanning machine which would show any cancer in the body. She had heard of such a machine in Sheffield, some eighty miles away.

At this time I was working as part-time secretary in two schools as well as doing two 'A' levels at a local further education college. The 'A' level course was a daytime one and very intensive, and I had quite a rush to get from the schools to college. I did have to miss a few lectures on Monday - dinner money collection at the schools - and I then had to copy notes from my fellow students who were the usual age group for 'A' levels, sixteen-eighteen, and who had no other commitments.

I also was very much enjoying the course and hadn't missed any of the lessons I could attend, yet my love for my friend prompted me to suggest a trip to one of our favourite old hunting grounds, Leek, a market town sitting on the edge of the Staffordshire Moorlands. She protested at my suggestion arguing that I couldn't afford to miss my lessons, but I would hear none of it.

Thank God I did. It was to be the last time we went to Leek, or out anywhere, for that matter, without being under the death sentence she was soon given.

At Leek, true to form, we found ourselves in peals of laughter while having lunch in our favourite pub. The landlady was a bit of a comic too and we soon had the whole snug bar in gales of laughter. It was a beautiful December day, crisp, with full sunshine, and the Salvation Army were playing Christmas carols in the bustling market square. I have a picture frozen in my mind of the steeple of a church on the drive home silhouetted against a brilliant blue sky, because at the time I told myself that this was a moment to treasure.

We had wanted this perfect day to last as long as possible so, before we had to get back to collect the children from school, we had called into a little tea-shop run by two sweet old ladies. Full of fun, we entered the cosy, sedate interior and we sat at the only available table. We had to behave well in here and so were not as raucous as earlier at lunch. A lady came in and as there were no spare tables she asked if she could sit at ours. We didn't mind one bit, and afterwards we laughed at what she must have thought of us because one minute she was sitting with two obviously happy people who were giggling together, causing her to smile, and the next minute she was with two women who held hands while tears of grief streamed down both their faces and they had to pay the bill and quickly leave the tea-shop.

The reason for the tears was that my friend had suddenly said that if the scan showed that the cancer had returned, she wanted me to have her wedding ring. She also made me promise that I wouldn't let her husband's father attend her funeral.

There was no need for the scan. She quickly became very ill and had to cancel her long-planned party as she was continually vomiting and she was soon in hospital undergoing tests which showed that she indeed had secondary cancer. I rang the hospital and asked to see the specialist whose care she was under, and, without anyone knowing I saw him in his office. My friend's distraught husband had told me that the secondary was in her kidneys, and I asked the doctor if he could use one of my kidneys if this would help to save her. He was a lovely, kind man, and was obviously moved by the love I showed for her, yet he quietly explained that as the cancer was in her liver an organ transplant would do no good.

I still clung to the hope that if anyone could beat this then she could, and she certainly did not lose her optimism. While vomiting every five minutes or so, she still managed to write me a note - this even though I visited nearly every day.

She wrote to me that she had decided to move house when she came out of hospital as she had never liked the one she lived in. She did have a short remission and she did view a lovely house which she was determined to buy.

At this point I had a dream. In the dream I was following her coffin into the porch of a church. I saw every detail from the flowers on top of the coffin to the barrel-vaulted ceiling of the porch. I awoke in great distress and decided that this dream was due to my subconscious playing with my unacknowledged fear of her dying. I knew that she was going to live, and my will power and hers would see her through.

I received a phone call from her niece at 3am on the 29th January, telling me that she thought my friend was dying. My husband and I sped to my friend's house to find that she had just died. I rushed to her prostrate body and felt her forehead which was still warm.

Something died in me that night. A light somewhere in my deep psyche went out, and, although I performed the duties of a support for her husband, who was in a state of collapse, I was not really living.

The week before she died, I had my husband drive past the church nearest her house in order to see if it had a porch like the one I had seen in my dream. Thank God it did not. It had a flat front with no porch. I had then clung even further to my hope that she would somehow pull through.

For the next week after her death I stayed with her husband during the day and my husband stayed with him during the night. He was in such a dreadfully shocked state, and we were concerned he might have done himself some harm. I was there while the undertaker made the necessary arrangements and was relieved to hear that she would be buried at the nearest church, which was the one my husband and I had driven past the week before she died. I didn't want the dream to be prophetic. In common with many other mothers I had nightmares of all sorts of accidents happening to my children which I certainly didn't wish to come true.

Yet on the day of the funeral I followed her coffin into the *interior porch* of the church exactly as in my dream.

CHAPTER SIX

Let the petty wishes for which you now approach God be realised or not, let the plans for promotion and progress which you place before God, be fulfilled or not; they are not so important after all. The primary aim should be to become Masters of yourselves, to hold intimate and constant communion with the Divine that is in you as well as in the Universe of which you are a part. Welcome disappointment, for they toughen you and test your fortitude.

- Sathya Sai Baba

IT TOOK NEARLY A YEAR for me to start to recover. I remember suddenly being aware of the vibrancy of trees and grass and the startling colour of the sky and realised that I had closed myself off to all the beauty in the earth from the time of her dying.

I continued my studies and the day came when I found myself driving to Keele University for my first day as an undergraduate. Again, this event is frozen in time, because I remember deliberately telling myself that this was a milestone and the 'first day of the rest of my life'. I seem to have had more than my fair share of these beginnings.

University life was wonderful. I threw myself into my studies and also got involved in everything I could. I was hungry for the stimulation of learning and loved being with such young people. I did everything from joining the Geography Society to sledging in the snow on dinner trays.

There is a belief at Keele in the Renaissance Man so that all subjects are tasted in the Foundation Year. I sat in wonder in the lecture theatre watching incredible pictures of the latest Voyager shots of the rings around Saturn as we started with astronomy, and was even thrilled to listen to the case of the snail in the ginger beer bottle when we learned about liability law.

I had had a vague notion when I first renewed my education a few years before and was thrilled to see the magical patterns in maths, that somehow learning was not simply a means of getting job qualifications, but was an end in itself. I had the strangest sense that learning was for life and that somehow it was what God wanted us to do. The only group I kept away from at Keele were what my fellow hall mates called, 'Those mad Christians.' There was a group of zealous 'born again Christians' who certainly were a bit manic and walked about with very serious faces and didn't join in the fun. I thought it rather sad that instead of attracting people to God they were, in fact, doing the opposite. Nobody wanted to be screwed up like the Christians. I did my little bit of publicity whenever the opportunity naturally arose and I shared my conviction that a loving God certainly did exist. I also by this time shared my 'near death' experience when appropriate.

From the time of my little visit to the 'other side' and the look of pity on my husband's face when I related the incident, I had told no-one except, of course, my dearest friend. About 10 years after the event Beryl told me of a book she had heard about which had just been published and which related experiences similar to mine. This book was *Life After Life* by Raymond Moody. It was still another few years before I eventually read the book and which confirmed my belief that I had not suffered a brain aberration due to shock or lack of oxygen, but had experienced a part of the great transition from life to death, or rather from life to life.

In answer to the critics who say that near death experiences are products of brain dysfunction, I can answer that in the many people I have since facilitated in guided imagery, no two people have had the same experience, yet in near death experiences there is a remarkable similarity. Another argument against the truth that the near-death experience is an actuality is that when some event is well documented, people may imagine that they too are experiencing uniquely, when in fact they are merely duplicating what has gone before. In my case, I had the experience in 1966 and Raymond Moody's book, which was the first book to report the phenomenon, was not published until 1978.

It is my belief that when God decides that our life needs a little realignment, He shows His Grace and arranges some event to set us on our progressive course. My jump start was the break-up of my family. My relationship with my husband had reached the stage where neither of us had anything left to say to the other. The crunch came after I graduated and was considering a career or further post-graduate work and our daughter left for University. I was extremely depressed at the loss of my University friends and lifestyle, and distraught that my daughter, who was also my best friend, wasn't at home, although of course I had encouraged her to flee the nest. My son was going through a difficult patch; he had been unemployed for four years, and we were not the best of friends at this time. My husband left the family home to live in a flat and I had to get off my bum and get a job, any job, as long as it paid the bills. After a spell with a secretarial agency I got a job on a temporary basis to help out a lovely man who was the owner of a ten-acre industrial estate in Stoke-on-Trent. I threw myself into creating order out of chaos, and I suspect that in the beginning the owner wished he had kept me under wraps as I moved my desk to join him and his partner in their boardroom while I had my office refurbished.

I thoroughly enjoyed the task. It was just what I needed to forget my painful private life. I would go to the office at 8am and work solidly without a break, sometimes not getting home till 8pm when I would simply collapse in front of the television too tired to think.

In retrospect I can see God's Hand in my life at this time. After graduating I had thought of a career in child psychology and I would never of my own volition have taken the estate job in the first place, and it certainly didn't look as though there was a future career for me. After about six months when I had set up the administration side and the building work was completed, I did decide that I must now think of a career. I had obtained a Certificate in Education whilst doing my degree and I now secured a job teaching 'A' level psychology at two local colleges of further education. These teaching posts were part-time - teaching 'A' levels even full-time involved only a few hours' actual teaching. I felt that I could still run the estate, especially as I had appointed a staff of four. I presented the owners with the choice of either allowing me to run the place on a part-time basis, or I would appoint a full-time person to replace me. They opted for the former and I again found myself dashing from the estate to college, leading a hectic life which suited my needs not only because I enjoyed being engaged, also because it stopped me from facing the fact that my life was a mess.

Events took a rather dramatic turn when the estate was sold to a London based plc property consortium, and I was also faced with a decision about whether to take a full-time teaching post or carry on in the same way.

I found teaching 'A' level psychology very unsatisfying. I felt I was having to teach what I felt were useless ideas regarding the study of the human soul. Psychology actually means psyche — soul, ology = study, and not much attention is paid to the soul, in fact it is denied by most psychologists.

I knew I should not be teaching when I heard myself ask a particularly bright pupil why she wanted to study such a useless subject. Not the right attitude for a teacher, yet I suspect one shared by quite a few.

I let it be known to the property company that I was considering a full-time post in a Secondary school, which would have meant teaching social studies and drama, I intended that this fact should slip through the grapevine to the managing director of the consortium. He called me to see him in his plush office and offered me the position of managing the whole estate rather than only the administration side. He also increased my salary by nearly four times the amount I was currently getting. I still thought this job was a stop gap until I could concentrate on my real career, possibly in child psychology, if I could afford to do post graduate training.

That was in November 1987, and I was still, in 1996, managing the estate albeit with different owners and more commercial property to look after ranging in distance from Margate to Dumfries. I used to fret when I started on my path of self-realisation about being in the business world, which was and still is regarded akin to the devil's workshop by a lot of people. God sent me on a business conference at Findhorn, the spiritual community in Scotland, to help me understand that instead of the break-up of business and the economic system prayed for by some I knew, what was needed was a change of heart which can only come gradually from the inside and not from economic collapse which would cause far greater distress in the world. I also knew that God had placed me in the right place at the right time and that I had my small part to play in bringing about the changes needed in the business scene. However, I digress once again, and my excuse is that I love to see God's work in my life, the pattern of which I can only see when I look back.

CHAPTER SEVEN

Mere mechanical existence does no credit to one's humanness. Human birth is immensely precious. Three things have to be observed as a mark of real humanness: Fear of sin, love of God and morality in society. People should refrain from sinful acts. The Sanskrit saying declares: 'Men desire the fruits of meritorious acts, but do not perform such acts. They do not desire the fruits of sinful deeds, but indulge in sinful acts.' When people develop purity in thought, word and deed, they will reap the fruits of good actions.

- Sathya Sai Baba

MY NEW ROLE MANAGING the estate single handed had been very daunting at first, and I had many a sleepless night worrying about some aspect or other and I also had panic attacks about not being able to cope. I nevertheless settled down to manage the property with my full concentration as if it were my own business. I have always regarded loyalty as one of the most important qualities and I know that the owners were appreciative of the work I did. They were also very generous as an expression of this. I had been going through one of my bouts of feeling that there must be something more to life than simply living when I happened to see a tiny article in

The Observer about a workshop for women being held at a venue just outside Leek in the Staffordshire Moorlands. Two things caught my attention. One was that I had never heard of a workshop being held so close to Stoke and the other was that the subject matter struck a chord. The workshop was based upon a book called 'Women Who Love Too Much', by Robin Norwood, whose hypothesis is that the reason women (and men for that matter, the title is misleading), cannot sustain a good relationship is that they are continually trying to resolve the conflicts from the original relationship with their parents.

At this time my relationship with my partner was going through a difficult patch and I could see the same pattern emerging as in my marriage. Thank God I didn't load all the blame onto my partner. I suspected at least a fifty-fifty chance that I too somehow played my part in the difficulties.

Now that I know a little more of God's planning I laugh when I think of what he did to make sure I went on this workshop. I sent the necessary stamped addressed envelope for an application form which duly arrived. Before I filled it in, however, the relationship reverted to its former loving self and my partner and I booked a romantic trip to Paris. I tore the application form up and threw it in my office bin. The Paris trip was a disaster, and I came back feeling awful and very annoyed with myself for not only throwing the application form away but also the newspaper cutting. Two days later another application form arrived in my post! I had never been to a workshop before and on the morning I was due to go I almost changed my mind. Thank God I didn't, as I see this as the event which started me onto my self-awareness/spiritual path which has shown me that there really is a purpose to life.

This workshop made me realise that I had a lot of emotional pain lying deep within which I had been suppressing all my life. It triggered the memory of a time when I was eleven and going through a particularly stressful time. I lay in bed wet, because I wet the bed frequently up to the age of fourteen, and thought that the only hope of my leading a normal life and functioning in the world and eventually becoming a wife and mother was for me to pretend I was OK and suppress the anguish I felt inside. This workshop also made me aware that the origins of my distress lay further back in childhood and may even have started as I lay in my mother's womb - a girl whose parents were preparing for a boy and had chosen only a boy's name and who was certainly not planned.

Just prior to this milestone, in October, 1988, I had already felt a restlessness which led me to enrol for two courses at Keele University. One was a painting class led by a local artist Arthur Berry who didn't really teach me how to draw and paint but whose enthusiasm for great art matched my own, and the other course was entitled 'An introductory guide to investments'. The latter was my attempt to understand a little of the economic aspect of the business world as at the board meetings held once a month in London, not only was I the only woman, I was also the only person among the fourteen board members who was not from the disciplines of law or surveying. I felt somewhat disadvantaged when yields and capital growth were discussed.

In the interim, between enrolling for the courses and their beginning, I went on the 'Women Who Love Too Much' workshop which changed my focus so much that I found myself sitting for the first lesson in 'Psychological Healing' a course run by Helen Graham, lecturer of psychology at Keele, while my partner had taken my place in the investment class.

Apart from this radical change of mind following the 'Women Who Love Too Much' workshop, the other surprising thing was that I had vowed never to be involved again in anything relating to psychology as taught in British universities and particularly at Keele. It had seemed that the one thing which the lay-man thinks psychology is about, namely what makes a human being tick, is precisely what is avoided by most psychology departments. I had seen Helen at Keele and had attended a few of her lectures and had been very impressed with both her professional approach and the contents of her courses, yet I had decided during study for my degree to make the best of a bad job in the psychology front and simply try to stifle my dissatisfaction and chosen courses less meaningful but more rote learnable

As I sat in the 'Psychological Healing' class I didn't think Helen had recognised me and I certainly didn't make myself known to her as I always disliked those sycophantic students who seemed to me to need special treatment. At the time I didn't realise that I too had a problem which was manifested by my attempt to cover up my neediness by appearing to be indifferent.

This workshop was another milestone in my spiritual development. Helen introduced me to the deep hidden depths of my soul through her use of guided imagery. I had studied the work of Carl and Stephanie Simonton on the use of guided imagery in the treatment of cancer patients during my degree years, but without the first-hand experience I received in Helen's course I had rejected the Simontons' work as being rather fanciful.

In the workshop I realised that I had a vast reservoir of previously untapped information which could help me in my attempt to uncover who I was and also perhaps give me a clue about the purpose of life.

It was during one of Helen's sessions that I met Tso Chi. We had been asked while deeply relaxed to visualise a face appearing in an imaginary cloud in the sky and I fully expected to imagine the face of Jesus as he was my only God type image. I was surprised, therefore, to see instead the impression of an old Chinese man with a long-pointed beard and a strange cushion type hat.

I have always been sceptical about mediums who claim to be in touch with spirits and from my experience earlier, when my dear friend and I used occasionally to visit spiritual church sessions, I felt my suspicions were well founded. It seemed to me that the medium was usually female and old and I suspected that most had not been listened to very much in their lives until they 'discovered' a talent for getting in touch with those departed. The information passed on was, or so it seemed to me, very nebulous, - most people attending such meetings being desperate to contact someone they were still grieving for and ready to believe the flimsiest evidence that they could be in touch. The medium would only have to say 'I have someone here whose name begins with an 'M' for a dozen hands to shoot up, hoping and praying that it was their particular lost Mary, Mavis, Michael, Marion etc. etc. etc. The rest was easy as the information usually provided from there on was so vague that it could apply to any number of people, yet some desperately grieving person would claim it as his or her own.

I once demonstrated to a group of BBC technicians, who were staying at the same hotel whilst I was on holiday in Crete and they were filming, how gullible even intelligent people can be if they want to believe something. I pretended to read their palms and used the same technique I had seen used by fortune tellers where I made a general statement and then waited till they fed me the answer. It went something like this:- I would say 'You are worried about something'. They would reply eagerly, 'Yes, my mother, job, etc'. I could proceed from there. At the end of this demonstration I came clean and told them that I could not read their palms and they themselves in their eagerness to have solutions to their problems had provided me with all the information I needed to appear clairvoyant. They did not believe me and insisted I really had told them things I could not have known. This showed me the extent of their mind. I am not saying that I thought all mediums and fortune tellers were deliberately faking. Although I actually know of one who made no pretence to her close friends that she duped people for money, but I believed that a lot of mediums simply use their creative imagination and believe their own publicity.

Until the time of my experience in Helen Graham's workshop I hadn't believed that non-living entities could be contacted, so you can imagine how reluctant I was to accept my Chinese 'friend' Tso Chi. I put him through hell in my attempt to find out if he was 'real' or a figment of my imagination. I had only just found that I could contact a part of me that had previously only been glimpsed in the dream state, and only from the view from higher up the mountain can I see that Tso Chi is an aspect of my higher soul self which has lived here on earth many times before.

At this time however I tested and tested the venerable gentleman. I remember lying under a cherry tree in Scotland - yes, I did see the connection between cherry blossom and China - and I closed my eyes and had an image in my inner scene. I don't always see clear pictures but I get the 'thought' of something. I saw Tso Chi and I asked him to prove to me that he really existed outside my imagination by showing me something I could not know about. He showed me an exquisite pair of tiny red silk damask slippers, and although I had not seen anything like these before, I said, 'No I know about the Chinese binding women's feet - show me something else.' He then showed me a finely detailed duck with all feathers perfectly outlined. It was beautiful and I thought at first it was finely carved from wood but then realised this was made of paper. Even so I would not accept this as I also knew about, origami although I had only seen very crude examples in book illustrations and nothing like this amazing duck. Again, I asked for something I could not possibly know about, and his patience was incredible. Why he didn't go away and give me up as a bad job is still a wonder to me. Instead, however, he showed me the making of an article which to this day I have never discovered its use. It started with a roll of parchment type paper which was heavily embossed with a Chinese type pattern. This parchment was then rolled up to form a tight roll and a sharp object inserted at one end.

I very reluctantly had to accept that Tso Chi was not made up by me, yet I was still uncomfortable about his appearance in my life. He explained that he had been a healer in 4th Century China, although the word healer as used in today's language does not fully explain his role. He wore very elaborate clothes, certainly not the kind I would have thought a holy type person would wear, more akin to a Chinese Emperor's and he showed me his place of healing.

When a person consulted him he looked at the whole person, not in separate compartments, but mind, body and spirituality combined. His task was to keep people from getting sick and he used whatever method was appropriate for each individual case. For some it would be a type of psychological counselling, although as he was quick to point out, not like we use in the west today where someone who has learned a few academic notions then imparts this rote learning onto the patient. The method used in his healing centre was of a much different kind. In order to do the work of helping people with emotional problems the healer had to be a very evolved person who had not only studied the ancient texts, but who had completely mastered the problems he would be helping with. Of course, this meant that not many people were master healers.

There was another way which he told me about which helped a lot of people, and this was for a couple of individuals to be put together and given the task of listening to each other without comment or interruption. Tso Chi said that many people suffered from lack of communication which led to feelings of isolation, and from there to sickness of mind followed by sickness of body. If the person had another who simply listened with full attention and interest then much of the stress of living could be alleviated before sickness developed. These ideas were certainly new to me at that time.

I kept very quiet about my Chinese teacher. He used to help me with information about what to suggest as treatment for those who came to me and poured out their troubles. I remember sitting in my office one day when my mother, who had cancer of the ovaries, was going to see a homeopathic doctor as a last resort, because the hospital doctors had tried all they could. I was very busy with my estate duties, so I simply connected for two seconds with Tso Chi who showed me what looked like a bunch of seaweed and who said 'Tell the doctor, seaweed.' I didn't know what this meant but as I was by this time more trusting of his advice, I intended to carry out his instructions.

Dr David Smallbone, the homeopathic doctor, is a remarkable man, and I had already had cause to be thankful for him when he got me back on my feet after a month in bed following a trip to Sri Lanka where I contracted a particularly nasty viral infection which my GP thought at first may have been malaria. I had also spoken to Dr Smallbone about my Chinese friend and as he is a very evolved person, he accepted this as quite 'normal'.

He gave my mother various treatments and advice and then paused while writing his prescription to check that he had thought of everything. I suddenly remembered Tso Chi's words and I told the doctor what my Chinese guide had said. I didn't look at my mother sitting next to me because I was embarrassed as she knew nothing of my guide and always scoffed at anything she could not experience with the five senses. She was, however, too ill to notice and was hardly aware of the exchange between the doctor and myself. He exclaimed, when I related the message, 'Of course, kelp,' and added this to the list of vitamins he was prescribing. I later read that kelp was being tested as a help to cancer patients and had received promising results.

CHAPTER EIGHT

Many people speak about getting a vision of God. This is a naive desire. They do not realise that the Divine is present in everything they see. The Vedas declared that man fails to see the Divine though the Divine is manifest in everything that he sees. The Vedas declared such a person a complete fool. Everything in the universe is permeated by the Divine. Everyone should seek to realise his/her divinity and recognise the divinity in all beings.

- Sathya Sai Baba

DURING THE TIME I was attending Helen Graham's workshop 'Psychological Healing', I experienced a phenomenon which I now know is my soul or higher self, bypassing my ego and putting ideas and words into my mouth which I didn't know I knew, and which are a great surprise to me. One of my fellow students was struggling with his new found connection to the soul, which he intuitively knew was God, and the conflicting views he had accepted as gospel from the church he attended. He was talking to Helen and myself one evening during coffee break about his dilemma and was coming down heavily on the side of the Church. I was surprised to hear myself say that God is above all religions and that the only purpose for religion is as a tool to enable man to have direct contact with God. Each religion, I argued, at its core preached this fundamental truth, but man, for reasons of ignorance, power and corruption, had mistaken the end. Wow! I didn't know I had such ideas, yet I knew in the very cells of my body that this was the truth.

I was now on what I call my conscious spiritual path. I believe we are all on our spiritual journey from the time we decide to incarnate in a human body, yet until the time some event jolts us into awareness, we are convinced that the world of the five senses in which we experience life is all there is.

Don't for a minute think that from this time I lived in constant spiritual awareness. I would say that the spiritual quest was a very small part of my life, taking a back seat most of the time to my working and private life. Unlike physical journeys, however, there was no turning back. Even when the going got rough, and it did get very rough at times, I still could not go back to the time when I was spiritually unconscious. At times I wished I could turn the clock back, because I found that I no longer had the taste for the things which had seemed so important before. I was bored with conversations about mundane affairs, and wanted to talk about the discoveries I was making in the metaphysical field. My love of life had increased although the emphasis had shifted away from artificial pursuits - I was no good at parties any more - to things that had always been important, but which now had an added depth, especially my love of nature

My taste in reading matter also changed dramatically at this time. I have always been an avid reader and my tastes ranged from the classics - I love Shakespeare and the Brontës - to any biography especially about sailing odysseys, but now I started to devour books on any metaphysical and self-help topics.

Stoke-on-Trent was not very well served for this type of book, even at the students' bookshop on the Keele campus, making me rely on a postal service provided by a very aptly named shop: 'Manifestations Unlimited'. Whenever I heard of a book I thought I would need, I sent off for it from the shop. I also raided any esoteric bookshop I found myself in, and once came back from a workshop at Findhorn weighed down with twenty-two books, only to find a parcel containing another three from my postal service. I read more books in one year than I had read in the four years of study for my degree where I was an enthusiastic student who did a lot of reading.

Because of my 'doubting Thomas' personality, God arranged my Spiritual degree in such a perfect way that He always allowed me to work something out until I had the realisation, and only then did He arrange for me to find the confirmation in a book. If it had happened the other way around, I would have been convinced that what I had discovered was simply borrowed from others' ideas and not from deep within myself.

After the Helen Graham course and my first taste of a workshop I then found myself drawn to Findhorn in Scotland. I had never heard of the place until Margaret Lyth, the lovely woman who ran the Women Who Love Too Much workshop, mentioned it.

The community was founded by a remarkable threesome: Eileen and David Caddy and Dorothy Maclean as a place where spirituality rather than religion can be practised as well as preached. They run various workshops ranging from Sacred Dance to Intuitive Diagnosis of Disease.

Every newcomer has to attend the Experience Week, and this is what I did. I loved the place. For the first time since I was a child, I re-experienced the thrill of wandering alone without a care in the world among the tiny paths in the magical gardens and, in great excitement, to walk to the ocean and the estuary. I connected to aspects of myself which I had suppressed since childhood when I had learned that in order to succeed and belong in the world, I had to squash my sensitivity and pretend to be as 'cold' as my fellows. I once again attuned to the nature elements as I had as a child and would sit for long stretches enjoying the life forces which I could feel and see in my inner scene. Then I got ill.

I started with an extremely sore throat which always heralds an attack of bronchitis, usually lasting for two weeks at least. I had a very high temperature and could not get out of bed. I felt that the bed would surely be burned under my furnace like body. The community members were wonderful caring people who came to visit me and administer various natural remedies which I had tried before and which were not effective in my case. Only antibiotics and the strongest my doctor prescribed did the trick and then only slowly. I used to get an attack twice a year and my mother said I 'cut every tooth with bronchitis' and I was used to raging fevers but nothing like this. The thought crossed my mind that maybe those crazy stories of people who have suffered spontaneous combustion were true after all, for I certainly felt this would happen to me.

The leader of my group came to visit and I remember him saying that sometimes God arranges this kind of 'baptism by fire'. I felt too ill to care and eventually I must have drifted off to sleep because I only know I woke the next morning with the fever gone and a wonderful cool feeling as though my blood had been cooled under a mountain stream. Every symptom had miraculously disappeared, and I felt such peace and bliss I can hardly describe. I decided not to join the group this day as they were not expecting me and I needed some time on my own. I borrowed an old bicycle from Julie, a lovely friend I had made who lived in the community, and I cycled along the sand dunes to the ocean.

The beach is very pebbly with huge, almost boulder like pebbles near to the dunes, and walking here is difficult and riding impossible, especially for me, as I didn't take much exercise. This morning, however, I felt as though my legs belonged to someone else. I was like the bionic woman who had dynamos inserted to give superhuman power. I could not normally have begun to ride over the beach if I was in full strength, and considering I had been so ill the day before I would have been surprised to have been able to walk there. I revelled in my new found strength and simply glided over the beach enjoying the crystal blue sky and the sparkling ocean. I felt like Goliath, and am sure I could have lifted a mountain if anyone needed me to. It is only with hindsight that I now know that this was a kundalini experience.

CHAPTER NINE

Remember that with every step, you are nearing God, and God, too, when you take one step towards Him takes ten towards you. There is no stopping place in this pilgrimage, it is one continuous journey, through day and night, through valley and desert, through tears and smiles, through death and birth, through tomb and womb. When the road ends, and the Goal is gained, the pilgrim finds that he had travelled only from himself to himself, that the way was long and lonesome, but the God that led him unto, was all the while in him, around him, with him, and beside him!

- Sathya Sai Baba

I ALWAYS TRY TO FIND A rational explanation for events. I have a sharply developed brain which has never been content to simply let things be but which loves to dig and delve until the unexplained is explained - at least to my satisfaction. I would have made a good detective. Sometime in the early 1980s, however, an event occurred for which even I could find no logical explanation.

I had a number of Roman Catholic friends - I worked as part-time secretary at two schools - one a

Church of England and the other Roman Catholic. I was comfortable with my Catholic friends, especially with my friend and neighbour Peggy Hogg. I was also intrigued by anything out of the ordinary and I jumped at the chance of joining a group, including Peg, who were going on a pilgrimage to The Holy Shrine of Our Lady at Lourdes. The history of Lourdes is that Our Lady appeared to Bernadette, a local village girl, and from this day pilgrims have been going to the shrine where a number of miracles - some even acknowledged by the Vatican - have taken place.

Again, I was cast in the role of doubting Thomas. I remember I was asked to take part in an interview, broadcast live on Radio Stoke, even though, or perhaps especially because, I was going with doubts as to the authenticity of the claims being made and not as a paid-up member of the Catholic church.

I cringe now as I remember replying to the interviewer's question about whether I would go into the healing waters. 'No way' I said would I be using the same water as people with weeping sores and other nasties. I have always been a fastidious kind of person and even at school I wouldn't use anyone else's comb and always made sure I used a clean section of the roller towel.

My mother and a couple of her friends were also in the group and with my friend Peg we made up quite a jolly group, more like holidaymakers than holy pilgrims. Sean Collins, a rather fanatical Catholic who devoted his life to taking pilgrims to

Lourdes was the organiser, and on the coach to the airport he asked me if I would step in the place of Lesley, a young mother about my age who had leukaemia and had intended to be on this trip, but who had to cancel at the last minute due to a setback in her condition.

I am ashamed to say that before I agreed I wanted to know what this entailed. It could have meant going into the baths, and Sean was very vague but assured me that I would not have to go into the water but would simply act as surrogate when holy candles were given to the sick. This didn't seem very painful, and in any case, I knew of Lesley - she was one of the staff at my hairdressers - and felt great compassion for a mother who had to face the likelihood of dying and leaving her young children.

We were in a small plane and when we hit a bit of turbulence it was like being on the big dipper at Blackpool, yet here we were, a gay bunch, and we spent our time joking and laughing and arrived at our *pension* in Lourdes tired but in very good spirits.

Peg and I shared a cosy room and we were going to share a bottle of wine we had brought as a night-cap, but decided we were too tired and so went to bed stone cold sober. I drifted off to sleep happy and looking forward to what the next day would bring.

I must have slept for an hour or so and was in a deep dreamless sleep when I was jolted awake by a severe cramp like pain across my chest. I could hardly breathe and I tried hard to calm my already frightened mind. My father had suffered a heart attack and I knew from him that the feeling was just like the constricting band of pain I was experiencing. Could I be having a heart attack? I was only in my early thirties, yet the pain was so severe. I didn't want to disturb Peg, yet without a sound from me, she woke and asked what was the matter. By this time, I started to experience a sensation like pins and needles in my feet and fingers and a creeping paralysis up my arms and legs. I didn't remember that this was similar to my experiences during my daughter's birth; all I knew was that I felt I was dying. My chattering teeth sounded like a spoon player and I was icy cold.

Peg, very much alarmed, got into bed with me in an attempt to try to get some warmth to my freezing body. She was very concerned and left me for a minute while she raced to fetch my mother who took one look at me and sent Peg to wake the madame of the *pension*.

The French woman knew no English, but she too was alarmed at the sight of me and quickly rang for a doctor. One of the priests in our party was also rudely woken from his sleep to act as interpreter, because the doctor also knew no English and, apart from being able to ask the time, which somehow didn't seem appropriate, I knew no French. In any case, I could not speak as my breathing was now harsh and had a distinct rattle and my teeth would not keep still. I didn't have an out of body experience - I only wish I had in order to escape the pain - but stayed conscious the whole time.

I was a little puzzled by the doctor's attitude. He felt my pulse and put his stethoscope on my chest and I knew that of course he would send me to hospital. Instead he simply said something to the priest and left. The priest interpreted and told us that the doctor was not concerned but would call on me the next day. My mother to whom any doctor is God, was satisfied with this, but I remember Peg being even more alarmed and trying to find out what the doctor had thought was the matter with me. This was to no avail, but luckily by this time my symptoms were slowly subsiding and I thought it just possible I might live to see another day.

The next morning after a deep refreshing sleep I woke feeling so well I could have run a marathon. I was so embarrassed by the attention I got from the others in my group who had heard of the fun and games during the night and were all concerned for my wellbeing. I told Peg that I felt at least I ought to limp so as not to appear a hypochondriac who had caused good people to miss their night's sleep. I am glad she was there to witness the whole thing, not only because she was loving and cared for me, but to confirm it really did happen and I had suffered so much.

Despite my loud protestations to the contrary on Radio Stoke, I did take the waters that day. I actually followed a poor lady with a very unsightly skin complaint, but felt so full of love and joy that I could have happily stayed in the waters with her for ever. The 'standing in' for Lesley only involved receiving a candle on her behalf, yet I threw myself wholeheartedly into my task and also walked the stations of the cross on behalf of Lesley following a similar path Jesus took to the crucifixion.

On my return home I went straight to the hospital where Lesley was staying, clutching the candle and some holy water and also a present from me. I felt a little stupid when the lovely staff nurse said she had been discharged and I was very surprised to hear myself relate the experiences I had had on the Friday night.

Why I told her this is one of the examples to me of those times when my soul seems to bypass my ego and speaks through me. I was acutely embarrassed and yet the staff nurse didn't react as I expected. Instead of the pitying look I thought she'd give to this mad woman clutching her gifts and babbling about nearly dying in Lourdes, she asked me to wait a minute while she looked at the charge book. This is the daily recording of events which take place on the ward. She returned to tell me that on the Friday night it had been recorded that Lesley went into crisis and fears were expressed for her life. During the night however she came through and the following day was so much better it was decided she could go home to spend what turned out to be the last precious time with her husband and children. I was stunned. Although the exact symptoms were not recorded the staff nurse said that Lesley could very well have suffered similar experiences as me hundreds of miles away in Lourdes.

God had, of course, arranged for this nurse, who was a religious person, to be on hand to help me understand what had taken place. I remember she said that God had placed Lesley in my hands and used me to effect a healing.

I am ashamed to say that although I was delighted that Lesley had gone home so much better, I didn't feel thrilled about anyone being 'laid in my hands'. It seemed at the time to be too much responsibility and altogether too strange. I just wanted a quiet time with my own family. Now I know a bit more, I understand that this event was an example of distant healing whereby God uses an individual as an instrument to heal another and distance is no barrier. I also understand that anyone can be used, even a doubting Thomas such as I, one who didn't believe in such happenings. In the case of Lesley and myself only a willingness on my part to act as a substitute and the genuine compassion which I felt for her predicament was all that was necessary.

CHAPTER TEN

What is the cause of droughts and floods which occur in the world? Man seeks to enjoy the benefits of Nature without any restraint or regulation. The result is imbalance in Nature which has grave consequences. Here you have a globe. If you hit it one way, its balance is disturbed. We should always see to it that in the utilisation of natural resources a proper balance is kept. Excessive use in any one direction will result in harm in another direction.

- Sathya Sai Baba

I HAVE ALREADY MENTIONED in passing that I had rough times as well as smooth and I would like to give an example of a particularly horrible rough time. It was in January, 1990, during the Gulf war. January is always a time for me of great depression. I think I suffer from lack of sunlight and also the psychological effect of the post-Christmas blues. From my present vantage point I can see that these times are very productive and a necessary part of my growth. The bulb has to spend time under the soil where it builds its strength in order to make the sprint for the surface and flowering. I see this analogy fits my January pattern. I want to pull the covers over my head and not go out and I really suffer but afterwards I emerge to a new 'flowering' of ideas and joy of life.

At the time of the Gulf war however I hadn't seen the positive and, in any case, when I am in the depression, it seems as though I'll always be that way. The Gulf war particularly depressed me even further. I was horrified that we humans were still fighting each other and man's inhumanity to man seemed to be as strong as ever. I also had my own little personal war going on in that I had my usual peaceful home environment disrupted by two young men who were lodging with me. One of them was a very negative person who, I felt, had a rather Svengali influence on the other, and I was concerned about the relationship. I discovered he had committed dishonourable acts and I felt that I had my own Saddam Hussain living under my own roof.

After a particular unsavoury experience when a very shady used car dealer had visited my home in connection with some 'scam' the young man was involved in, I felt that enough was enough, and I arranged for one young man to live with his mother while the other, even though he had parents who were willing to have him back with them, sat on my garden wall trying to look pathetic, pretending he had nowhere to go.

I remember clearly one morning when the war news was particularly inhumane, that I thought I didn't want to stay around any longer. I had no fear of dying and I knew by this time about reincarnation;

I thought I would opt out now and come back in a thousand years' time when the world will be a more loving place. I had read of the ancients who, when they felt their time was ripe for departure, could simply close their eyes, and die and I thought I would try this. I lay in bed without food or drink and with my curtains closed and the phone off the hook all day. My partner called to see me when he came home from work and he told me afterwards that I made a good corpse and really looked as though I was dying. My face was ashen and he said that if he had folded my hands and sent for Clem McGough, the local undertaker, no one would have been surprised. From past experience he knew it was no use arguing with me and he left me to it. I lay like this all night and the following day was prepared for another day, still determined to die.

About a year before this event I had started to read a book called *A Course in Miracles*, which I found to be a wonderful help on my spiritual journey. The book is in three sections: the first part, the text, then 365 lessons with the third part the teacher's manual. Never doing things the conventional way, I had been reading all three sections at once, and had consequently placed three bookmarks, one in each section, I had not opened the book since the previous November, and it now lay with a pile of other books on the large table in my bedroom.

As I lay this second day waiting to die I heard a prompting voice inside my head say, 'Go and look at the *Course in Miracles*. No way! I was waiting to die, wasn't I, and was not prepared to start reading. The inner prompting however was very strong and so like a naughty child I stomped out of bed and found the 'Course' under the pile of books. I blindly opened it at one of the three marked places, which happened to be the text, and let my pouting glance fall on words which said something like the following: 'So you want to die, do you? Well, death is an illusion, so get up and learn your lessons.'

What a shock. I jumped about three feet into the air and turned around a few times, a perfect example of the proverbial headless chicken syndrome, and I quickly raced to the bathroom to shower. Literally ten minutes later I was showered, dressed and sitting at the wheel of my car driving to the office. When my partner came to visit the invalid again after work, instead of the corpse, he found a vibrant woman who was gaily preparing a meal for them both and full of the events of a busy working day.

This incident is a classic example of the way God communicates with us if only we keep all channels open and are prepared to see lessons and advice in every situation. I believe that even the tiniest apparently mundane event has the potential to be the trigger for our greatest growth in self-awareness which I know leads to God. At the core of our being we are made of the same stuff as God. When we start to become aware of what makes us tick, because what makes us tick is God, we naturally realise that we are part of God, and we then know that there is no difference between us at the very centre of our being. Of course, a lot of pain and work is needed for this realisation. The ego self, whose very job is to make us separate and to guard and protect our privacy, is not going to give up easily because its death is the goal and its fight for survival is a very strong force.

I am, however, jumping ahead of myself. I certainly didn't have the above understanding when I tried to die, yet I now know that God knew everything that went on with me and communicated to me through books. I have already mentioned the fact that I was devouring philosophical, theosophical, psychological and self-help books and that I came back from a workshop in Findhorn weighed down with twenty-two such volumes. I hardly remembered what the titles of the books were and simply placed these, together with the other three, which had arrived by post, on my already groaning bookshelves.

My usual pattern is to be reading at least three at any one time, and when I finish a book I stand in front of my bookshelves and let my inner wisdom draw out a new one. I am fascinated that the new book always holds some gem for me that I need at that particular time. I have also already explained that the pattern is for me to struggle with a particular concept on my own, during reflection and/or meditation, until I get the understanding and then, as confirmation, to read this in a book. It had to be this way for me so that I could be sure I hadn't simply 'borrowed' someone else's ideas. I was also helped by my partner, although the help seemed like hindrance in the beginning. He is a very logical British academic and has very set ideas about the way the world runs, which does not include anything as 'airy fairy' as God. He is a very caring man and if he has to call himself anything, I think he would call himself a humanist.

I think he was genuinely concerned that I had lost a few of my marbles when I first started to bombard him with my new found ideas about the way the world really turns. He was very critical and this caused me a lot of pain because I could see that I would be treading a different path to him and our loving relationship may not have survived. I desperately wanted him at least to consider the ideas I was exploring but he saw it all as so much stuff and nonsense and actually said he found 'examining the navel' rather pointless and tedious to boot.

With hindsight I can see how God arranged for me to be with him exactly as he was. I needed to keep my feet firmly on the ground while my soul went soaring through the universe, and what better way to be really clear about what holds true than to have it picked to pieces by someone else. Truth will hold against all arguments and I am so grateful to him for the chance to eliminate the waffle and the crazy. I also see that God arranged for me to do my searching on my own. With no one to talk about my discoveries, I was able to keep the energy intact and allow the deep penetration of the lessons I was learning. I love him even more now than I did before and I thank him from the depths of my soul for the help he has given me.

CHAPTER ELEVEN

I am prepared to do anything for the good of the people. That is my only concern. I am working only to make the people worthy of the Lord's grace. Few people recognise this fact. Even those who have been coming to me for years do not recognise this truth. It is difficult to comprehend the truth about the ways of the Divine. All of you should attend to your duties with faith in the Divine, all will be well with you. You can accomplish everything with ease.

- Sathya Sai Baba

I STOOD IN FRONT OF MY bookshelves in a receptive state and reached for one of the unread books. The one my hand pulled out was one of the twenty-two brought back from Findhorn months before. It had the picture of a strange looking man with an Afro hairdo and was called *Transformation of the Heart.* I flicked through the pages and saw the name Sri Sathya Sai Baba. Where had I heard that name before? I then remembered that when I had earlier read a wonderful book written by Phyllis Krystal, a fellow psychologist, I had been surprised to note that she had dedicated the book to her guru, Sathya Sai Baba. I remember thinking how strange that an obviously intelligent woman should have a guru. I think a lot of people in the West have a very negative image of the guru concept and no wonder when all we hear is of strange sects who brainwash their devotees and won't let them leave the group. There have been so many stories of parents anxiously trying to reclaim their lost teenage children and the shocking case of the Jones people who committed suicide at the command of their guru hardly endears anyone to the phenomenon. As a free spirit and free thinker, I also didn't like the idea of someone telling me what to think and do as I imagined this was what gurus did. I was surprised therefore that I had bought this book at Findhorn but trusting that it would hold some information which I could use. Even if only to confirm my worst suspicions about gurus, I started to read.

The book is a collection of experiences of American devotees and I had only read the first chapter when tears started to stream down my face. The shock of my reaction stays with me even now. I felt a wave of electricity surge through my legs and arms and I just 'knew' that I had met God again, this time in the form of Bhagavan Sri Sathya Sai Baba.

I am an extremely fast reader but it took me ages to read this book. I would read a couple of paragraphs and have to put it down while I cried my eyes out. I felt as though my soul had returned from its wandering in the desert and been returned to its home. Every feeling of pain and loss I had ever experienced in my life seemed to burst forth to be expressed, released and then cleansed. I felt the tenderest love a mother has for her child gently wash away my tears and I knew that my search was over and that I was restored to my rightful place in the world and in heaven. Although I had been moved to tears by other beautiful words, especially the metaphysical poems of George Herbert, I had never before experienced anything like this.

I used to send my sister any book which I thought she might enjoy, so eventually without telling her of my experiences, I simply posted the book for her to read. Two days later, on the day she received it, she rang me in great excitement and said, 'Val, this is God.' Although I didn't need my experience validating, it was nevertheless good to have her share my knowledge. I had an overwhelming longing to see this God/Guru and I prayed day and night that He would let me visit Him in India.

I don't know how I knew, but somehow the formless God I had experienced when I 'died' giving birth to my daughter and then experienced as a light in the chapel and again whilst peeling potatoes, were one and the same as this Guru who lived in India. Again, because of the way God arranges things for me, He gave me experiences first and then let me learn of them afterwards in books. He also arranged for me to hear from others' experiences in order to give me confirmation that I was not alone in what were pretty astounding happenings.

The first of these unusual events was that one day I walked into my bedroom after a particularly difficult day at the office and smelled a beautiful sweet smell. The scent was not one with which I was familiar, and my first thought was that my cleaner had used a new polish and then I remembered that she wasn't due until the next day. I forgot about this incident until I again smelled the same sweet smell and this time in my garden, yet although I had a number of flowers in bloom this scent was unfamiliar and was in fact rather heady and exotic. I certainly didn't have anything like this among my English garden flowers. This, I later learned, is Sai Baba's way of communicating His presence.

The next unusual event in my life had its beginning a few years before this time. Around 1988 my mother told me one day that she was concerned about a problem she had had for some time. Every time she went to the toilet there was a copious amount of blood in the pan. I asked her where this was coming from and only those people with a mother like mine who had been brought up by a Victorian will believe that she didn't know. She told me she had previously been to the doctor who said it was nothing to worry about. I quickly arranged a private appointment with the gynaecologist and two days later we both listened in horror as he confirmed our fears. He could feel a large growth around her ovaries. She had the 'silent killer', ovarian cancer.

I took her home from the gynaecologists and she was in a dreadful state, so much so that she consented to my offer to help her relax using guided imagery to help her to cope at the time and through the coming events.

She had never allowed me to do anything like this before, protesting that she couldn't relax and that she had once been rejected by a stage hypnotist as someone too nervy and therefore unsuitable for hypnosis.

She very quickly relaxed this day as she lay on the hearth rug in her lounge with her head turned away from the chair I was sitting on. I could tell by her deep slow breathing that she was in the beta state and deeply unconscious.

I was, of course, also in need of help, and while she was lying there, I prayed to God to help her. I then 'heard' a voice inside my head rather like a thought which said, 'Put your hands on your mother.' Well, I wasn't going to do any such thing. If I had, it would have disturbed her and not only would it be harmful to her to be woken quickly I also knew that she needed this deep relaxation. In any case, I didn't know how or where to put my hands. I had heard of 'hands on healing', but had never seen it done. So I simply sat there. Once again the command came, 'Put your hands on your mother.' This time I would obey.

I remembered seeing Mickey Mouse in *The Sorcerer's Apprentice*, and I now thought of the wizard who had zigzags of lightning coming from his fingertips. I very quietly raised myself from my chair and bent down to my prostrate mother and because I didn't want to disturb her, I placed my fingers about two inches away from her body. As I knew the growth was in the ovarian region I concentrated on her pelvis. I had only just hovered over her with rigid wizard hands outstretched, and certainly didn't touch her or make a noise, when she suddenly jumped from her deep state and spun her head round in alarm. I assured her that all was well and she told me she had felt an intense burning in the region of her ovaries which interrupted a very pleasant-dream like state in which she imagined herself on a favourite beach. I then explained why her daughter had been crouched over her with fingers outstretched as though about to turn her into a frog like all good wizards do.

From this time on my mother and I would sneak into any odd corner we could find, especially tricky in the hospital where she had an operation to remove her womb and ovaries. I warned her not to tell anyone what we were doing because I was not comfortable in my new role as 'healer'. I would have done anything to help my mother, in fact, when she had chemotherapy, my hair fell out in lumps and she never lost a hair. I only subsequently realised that subconsciously I also tried to have cancer instead of her, and found myself with a seriously deficient immune system a year later. This is now known to be the fertile condition for abnormal cell growth to occur. Also, I didn't feel worthy, as I imagined healers needed to be akin to saints and I certainly had a lot of unsaintly attributes.

The gynaecologist asked me to tell my mother the dreaded news that she had advanced cancer and that the prognosis was dire. She took this very calmly, but that night she almost died. I asked if I could stay with her the next night but the hospital said they were sure she was over the crisis and were not happy to allow people to stay. This was because the ward my mother was in was a large one in an old hospital and had no facilities for extra 'unnecessary' night guests. They did, however, promise to ring me in the event of an emergency and so I left feeling a little comforted. My mother had also recovered greatly and this was the deciding factor.

That night I slept soundly. The previous week had been very stressful and I really needed my sleep. I was abruptly awoken, however, at about 1am and just 'knew' that my mother was in trouble again. I quickly got to the phone and rang the ward. The night sister said she had been about to ring me and that she had also called the duty doctor as she was concerned about mum. I raced back to my bedroom and grabbed my clothes. I had to get there fast. On my dressing table at this particular time I had some crystals in a group. I had only just got them and knew very little about them. Even though I was in a panic to get ready and get to the hospital, an inner prompting caused me to look at the crystals, and I quickly chose a single ended quartz stone and a lump of rose quartz. Why, I hadn't the faintest idea, but I was not thinking in a logical way, I was simply following my intuition.

I arrived at the hospital at the same time as the doctor who had probably been on duty for days and had been having a well-earned rest. The staff nurse had pulled the curtains around mum's bed who simply lay with a deathly pallor. I hesitated outside the curtains but the doctor waved me in and I was allowed to hold mum's hand while he examined her. He then took the staff nurse to one side, and while they went into a whispered huddle, I placed the single quartz under the covers by the side of the bed, about level with her navel, with the point facing away from her body and the rose quartz I placed higher up level with her chest. She was breathing in a shallow way and seemed unconscious.

The doctor was an angel, and without my having to ask, he called me to the desk opposite my mother's bed and screened from the rest of the sleeping ward. His fears were that she might suffer a cardiac arrest and there was also concern about renal failure. She was simply not passing any urine through the catheter fixed to her bladder. While I sat praying by her side with the crystals still hidden under the sheets, I really wasn't wondering why I had brought them because I was too distressed. I remember the staff nurse came to check on her and saw them, and instead of the disapproval I would have expected, she told me that her husband had been terminally ill and she had witnessed a miracle in his recovery which defied all the medical knowledge she knew. 'God works in mysterious ways,' she said.

The next two hours seemed like a lifetime as I sat with mum not knowing whether she would die or not. Both the doctor and staff nurse constantly monitored her until eventually the crisis was over. Her catheter started filling up and the doctor said she was now out of danger.

Not until much later when I came across a book about crystal healing did I discover that the rose quartz is for the heart. Unknowingly I had placed this at her chest region - and the single quartz is what is used to draw energy flow from the body. This I had again unknowingly placed just in the right position to help draw fluid from my mother's kidneys.

To me this is strong evidence for the efficacy of crystal healing as well as intuitive knowledge. I did not know about the crystals before this incident and even if I had known, my mind was not in a planning mood as I rushed to get ready for the nocturnal dash to the hospital. Again, if I had knowledge of the crystals before this, how did I know to pick the two out of the whole pile which were of specific use in the areas of concern, namely heart attack and renal failure All this while I was home getting ready and before even the doctor had seen her in the hospital to ascertain her problems.

The following day my mother was distressed and I asked her if she would like me to spend the night with her. I had already spoken to the lovely evening staff nurse and she had said this would be allowed and even suggested that a bed may be available for me. I slept a little during the day, and that evening I was prepared for my vigil. When I arrived at the ward it was obvious that the new rota staff were not thrilled that I would be there all night. I expect they thought I would hinder what was already a difficult job of looking after a large ward of postoperative patients and they were, of course, understaffed. The comfortable chair which had been there the night before had been replaced by a hard, plastic one, and yet I was so pleased to be able to be with my mother and fully sympathetic to the staff, that I decided a low profile was best, and so quietly took my place by my mother's bedside.

Along with the rest of the ward she was very restless. She was in considerable physical pain and was also disturbed by the noise coming from a dear old lady who, although she was at the far end of the ward, nevertheless could be heard loud and clear calling every few minutes for the nurses. The old lady was in great distress because she felt that she wanted to pass urine all the time and so was continually in fear of wetting the bed. The nurses responded occasionally but they were far too busy with problems on the men's ward on the opposite corridor to pay too much attention to her. She was, of course, disturbing the whole ward and I felt great compassion for these women who were in pain and in desperate need of a good night's sleep.

I timidly paid the old lady a visit prompted by my mother, timid because of the low profile I was supposed to be keeping. She was very distressed and was badly in need of someone to comfort her. I simply held her hand and listened to what she had to say and then lay my hand on her forehead and said a silent prayer for God to comfort her. I tiptoed back to my mother who was still in pain and asked her if she wanted some healing. Her bed was at the end of the ward nearest the door so she had a wall on one side and the screens were drawn on the other and at the end of her bed, so I felt we were safe to conduct our secret activity.

Mum did want healing, so I stood over her while she lay on her side with head away from me as this was how she was most comfortable. I was still at the Mickey Mouse wizard stage and I held my arms and fingers so stiffly that I had a very tense painful neck and shoulders. Of course, this was a small price to pay for what was obviously bringing relief to Mum. I placed my fingers as usual about two inches from her body and roughly in the pelvic region and started to pray to God to send healing through me to her. Nothing could have prepared me for the next event. I felt myself being lifted up into the air although I couldn't feel any pressure on any particular part of my body as you would expect from being lifted by another person's hands. It was a sensation of how I would imagine a feather feels blown into the air by a vacuum cleaner.

My first reaction was panic and then I heard a voice inside my head say, 'Calm, you know what this is'. I then relaxed and observed in fascination as my arms were taken over and made to make long sweeping movements, like a Geiger counter, over the whole of my mother's body. I don't know how long this lasted, probably only a few minutes, but when it was over I felt myself once again firmly on the ground. I then sank into the hard chair and had the most wonderful, calm, blissful feeling. My mother had stopped her restless movements and now slept like a contented baby. I could see a lot of the rest of the ward from around the curtains at the end of her bed, and I now noticed that the previously restless ward had also calmed and there was a gentle sound of soft breathing. The old lady was also quiet for the first time and the thought came to mind: 'The peace that passeth all understanding.' I knew that

God was in the ward and I felt I could have been happy to stay there forever.

Another remarkable thing happened. I have already said that the evening nursing staff were not happy for me to be there and had in fact changed the comfortable armchair for a hard one. As I sat in bliss on the hard chair the young staff nurse popped her head around the corner and asked if I would like a cup of tea. I said I would love one, but only if they had the time. After the tea I was offered a bed in a side ward which I thanked her for but refused preferring to stay in this God-filled ward and ready in case mum woke up. She then brought in the comfy armchair to replace the hard one and supplied a generous amount of blankets and pillows. What a change, and what had made the difference? I know that in some way the hearts of the staff were affected by the miraculous presence without necessarily knowing why.

CHAPTER TWELVE

Have no thorn of hate in your mind, develop love towards all. Desire is a storm, greed is a whirlpool, pride is a precipice, attachment is an avalanche, egoism is a volcano. Keep these things away so that when you recite the name of God or do Meditation, they do not disturb the equanimity. Let love be enthroned in your heart. Then, there will be sunshine and cool breezes and gurgling waters of contentment feeding the rocks of faith.

- Sathya Sai Baba

THE INITIAL PROGNOSIS WAS that my mother could not live much more than a few months; she did in fact live for two more years, and I believe that by God's grace she was given this time in order to resolve a few of the issues she had previously ignored. When she was dying, although she had protested all her life that there was no such thing as God, she actually asked me how to pray only hours before she died a very peaceful death. We had lit a candle when we knew the time was near and as she took her last breath the candle also burned its last.

Once again God had planned events with perfect timing in my life. About a year earlier I had heard through a friend about Elizabeth Kubler-Ross who at the time ran workshops on issues around death and dying. I had already read of these workshops and as I was eager for anything which helped my development. I had rung the organiser, a wonderful English lavender and lace lady called Ruth Oliver. She sent me an application form which I duly returned and secured myself a place on the workshop in twelve months' time! I was very lucky to have this place; the workshops were always over-subscribed as only one per year, or sometimes every other year, was held in the UK.

I remember attending a one-day workshop in London held by Phyllis Krystal, again booked months ahead. This was the week before mum died and I dashed from her bedside to attend the workshop and then quickly dashed back again.

At the Phyllis Krystal workshop I met a girl I had previously encountered at Findhorn, and she introduced me to Colin Caffell, who at that time was a trainee facilitator with Elizabeth Kubler-Ross. I remember telling Colin that I was booked on the course to be held in Edinburgh, but that as my mother was seriously ill, I didn't think I could attend as I would not leave her for any length of time.

Mum died on Tuesday the 6th June; her funeral was Wednesday, 13th June, and the Workshop began the following week. The timing was perfect - it would have taken me ages to release the grief of losing my mother, because I had already gone into denial and thrown myself into my work. Instead, because of the workshop, I cried solidly for three days and three nights.

At the Elizabeth Kubler-Ross workshop I had another example of the omnipresence of Sai Baba. I was so desperately unhappy and I gave Him a test. I asked Him to help me and to let me know He was with me. I sat at the meat eaters' side of the canteen. I was in good company because Elizabeth sat here too. I was feeling very wretched when a sparkling woman I had seen around but not spoken to came over to me and asked if my name was Valerie. I said it was and she then told me that she had had a dream in which Sai Baba said she must speak to me and that He wanted me to know He was with me.

I don't know who was most shocked, I at what she said, or she when I burst into tears in the crowded dining room. This lovely woman, Pat, is a close friend of mine now, and she can hardly remember the details of the incident as so much happened to her at the very intensive workshop. She does still remember my reaction though which of course surprised her because she didn't know I had asked Baba for proof that He was with me.

In retrospect, I can see His guiding hand in my painful process of self-discovery. Of course, because we all have the choice of free will and because no one else can do the discovering for us, I had to do the work myself. I fluctuated between periods of extreme bliss where I felt every day to be a blessing and felt the love of God all around me, to periods of intense pain and anguish in which all hope had gone and I was plunged into the depths of despair. I had so many 'dark nights of the soul' that I felt I could get a job as an usherette there. I believe that if He thinks a little outside help is needed, He arranges for that help and in my particular case this came in a peculiar way.

I have never been good in organisations and committees, much preferring to do something other than to talk about doing it, which was my previous experience of committee meetings. I also had little patience for the parade of egos which is also prevalent when some people get into minor positions of authority, and my attitude to rules which make no sense had always been to ignore them. I was therefore not inclined to seek out a Sai group and in any case there was not one in Stoke as far as I knew.

Baba, however, had decided I needed to experience other devotees, and one day I was sitting in my office reading through the mail my secretary had already opened, and opening the ones which said 'private', when I came across a strange circular. This was informing me that there was to be a meeting of Sai Devotees in the Isle of Wight and enclosing an application form plus details of ferry crossings and accommodation. To begin with, how did anyone know me when I had not been to a meeting, and secondly why had it been sent to my office and not my home where of course I received private correspondence?

I was most intrigued and that evening I rang the organiser. I was surprised that, unlike me, she didn't seem to be interested in solving the mystery. She said she couldn't remember sending it out, and therefore couldn't tell me from where she had had the address. She did say that similar unaccountable things had happened before and one had to accept this when dealing with Sai Baba. Although this certainly did not satisfy my detective brain, there was nothing I could do, and so I left the mystery unsolved and booked myself into the first Sai meeting in the Isle of White.

My sister came with me and we had a wonderful time. Unknown to me, Pat, my new friend from the Elizabeth Kubler-Ross workshop, was also there, although she, too, was very new to Baba and she had a friend with her. The four of us sat enthralled as we listened to a medical doctor who had been with Baba for years and who had wonderful accounts of Baba's love and service to humanity. Whilst watching this man, I noticed that his right hand and part of his arm had turned a vibrant green colour, and I knew this to be a sign that he was a healer because I had seen it a few times before on people who were doing healing work. While I sat there engrossed in the lecture theatre with my friends, I smelled the same smell that I had smelled in my house and garden but now I knew it to be the signature of Sai Baba. He leaves this wonderful sweet smell as a sign to let you know that He is always present. I looked at my sister who was crinkling her nose and she gave me a great smile. I looked to my other side and motioned to Pat and her friend and they too sniffed and nodded. When the doctor had finished his inspiring talk, the whole auditorium had to file out around the back of the stage in order to take tea in the garden, and as we got level with the stage the smell was even more intense. Baba was certainly letting us know he was there and for me it was wonderful to have witnessed this miracle in the company of others, rather than on my own.

I found from this first Sai Baba meeting that there wasn't a group in Stoke, but there was one in Sandbach, about 20 miles from my home. I rang the organiser, a wonderful devout and humble man, who works so hard for Baba, named Bal Unithan, and we had a good talk over the phone. He invited me to attend the next meeting and asked me to speak, at this meeting, about how I had come to hear of Baba. I was a little nervous about this, but he assured me that it was a very small friendly group of devotees, and so I agreed. I didn't prepare any notes as I really didn't have a lot to say and I could remember everything very clearly. Just as Bal said, the group was very friendly. I think there were about twenty people present and I simply talked from my seat.

A few weeks later Bal invited me to travel with his wife and mother to a meeting in Leeds, and again I agreed to talk of my experiences in getting to hear of Baba. It was summer and a hot day and I remember thinking that a simple cotton dress would be the most comfortable and I went with no tights and flat comfy shoes and very little make-up. You can imagine the shock when I found myself on a high stage complete with microphone in front of an audience of five hundred, and without notes. I felt sick. As I stood in the wings waiting for my turn I suddenly thought of Baba and I made a pact with Him. 'OK, Baba,' I said, 'you obviously got me into this, now please get me out.' I walked in front of the lights, took a deep breath and let Him do the talking. I know I said something which was meaningful because a number of people came up to me afterwards and said their hearts had been touched, but the embarrassing thing was, I didn't know what I had said.

I now realise that Baba was gradually getting me used to public speaking, because I was asked to speak at a couple of local venues and then He landed me with the big one.

Mrs Rajas Shiva Yogan, who was then head of the Sai Organisation in the UK. asked me to speak in London. I was on a stage with an even larger audience, with no notes, and again I asked Baba to speak through me. There was one horrifying moment when I tuned in to what I was saying and heard myself burbling on about EuroDisney. My ego took control and I almost dried up. I quickly 'plugged' into Baba, however, and all was well. At least I think it was. I don't know to this day what I said, and I had to leave the meeting as soon as I finished my talk in order to catch the train home.

As most good teachers know, and all good mothers, the way to teach a child a new skill is to start her off slowly and gradually with practice to build on the skill, This is exactly what Sai Baba did with me. He had started my public speaking activities with the small group at Sandbach and had then gradually given me larger and larger groups. Although I was gaining confidence and trust that He would speak through me, nevertheless it was still a nerve-wracking experience for me and not one I relished.

That same year Bal Unithan told me about the Crewe Retreat, which is a weekend meeting of Sai devotees and is the nearest thing to Puttaparthi (Sai Baba's Ashram in India) in the UK. The Retreat is held at Alsager, very close to my home, and I very excitedly prepared for my first visit. The event is very well organised and speakers are arranged in advance and are in such numbers that even the most important are strictly timed so that everyone gets to hear what each has to say. As I sat on the front row looking up at the beautifully arranged stage and listening to the excellent speakers, all devout and some very humorous, I remember thinking, 'Thank God I don't have to be up there and speak in front of this audience, which numbered about a thousand.'

Baba had other plans! He is a great trickster and He must have thought He'd have some fun with me. We had just been asked to decide which of three study groups we wanted to join and had been given the titles. I knew immediately that I should be in the one studying 'Detachment', but when we were allocated rooms and I saw that Detachment was in another building, which meant a short trek in the rain, I'm afraid I decided to opt instead for the one which stayed in the warm and cosy hall. I felt very uncomfortable, however, as I lazily sat in the warm seat I had occupied from the beginning because, of course, I had chosen for the wrong reasons.

I could stand the guilt no longer, so I made my apologies to the group teacher and raced across the yard to the meeting on 'Detachment'. Every seat was taken when I got there and the only place for me was on the front bench by the teacher. Why can I never slip in to the back when I've done something wrong! The class had started and I was informed that a volunteer had been called for to act as scribe. I was a little surprised at the reluctance of the group to do this as I had already found that Sai devotees are usually most anxious to serve. As I was on the front row and use shorthand, I thought I might as well do it. The talk given by Krishnan Kaul was very informative, and I thought I would type the thing at my own leisure and send a copy to anyone who wanted it.

Imagine the shock I got when Krishnan asked me if I was happy acting as spokesperson for the group and giving a précis of the discussion on the stage. I nearly fell from my chair. I hadn't realised that the scribe had to go up onto that frightening rostrum and talk. So that explained the lack of volunteers. I knew immediately that it was a Baba joke played on me because I had said I was glad I didn't have to speak and also to encourage me to conquer my fears about public speaking. Gentle Mother that He is, He did give me a chance to back out when Krishnan, who must have taken pity on my stricken face, said he would do it for me if I didn't want to. I knew this was a test and so I said I would give the précis. What I didn't tell him was that there was no way I could read what I had written as I had forgotten my glasses and also needed to put the scribble into some order. I also knew by now that

Baba wants to speak through me so I never know what words will come out of my mouth.

The audience was in uproar when I got to the microphone and told them of the latest little trick of the Great Trickster. I know that I didn't say anything about detachment, but was aware the word LOVE got a lot of airing.

CHAPTER THIRTEEN

The mere form of a human being is not significant. What is essential is the observance of human values. Men exhibit external changes, but there is no mental transformation. Many people come repeatedly to Puttaparthi. Physically they have changed, but there is no change in their mental outlook. Without such transformation man ceases to be human.

The Divinity in each human being will become manifest the day each one recognises the Divinity in every being. You must all realise the supreme sacredness of human birth. The qualities of forbearance, love and broad mindedness should germinate in every human being.

- Sathya Sai Baba

I DON'T KNOW WHEN I first had the thought that I wanted to go to India. All my life I have held a secret longing to visit. I have loved books and films set in this part of the world and Rudyard Kipling's book *Kim* is a book I get 'lost' in. I love all things Indian: food, music, temples, art and artefacts, and I also feel most at home with Indian people. It somehow feels to me as though I am with my dearest close family.

I remember that I met Amy Levy, the next Sai UK President, at the Isle of Wight meeting and asked if I could go with the group he was taking that October. This trip was fully booked and I tried to get on another group but this also proved fruitless. It is said that no one can go to visit Sai Baba unless He wants them to, and only in His time, and there are many stories of people's sometimes desperate yet abortive attempts.

I experienced this phenomenon in 1994 when I tried to go to Kodaikanal, Sai Baba's mountain retreat. I worked for Asian businessmen and had asked them if they would arrange my trip to Kodai through their travel agents. This they were kindly doing and I was all set to go when, just three weeks before, I went for the results of a routine chest x-ray only to be told by the chest consultant that there was cause for alarm, not from the results of the chest x-ray, but from the ECG heart test which had been taken as a matter of course. She said I needed to see a heart specialist immediately. There then followed a battery of tests ending in a very unpleasant intrusive heart investigation where I watched with fascinated horror on a VDU screen the fine camera tube exploring my pumping heart. The heart surgeon nearly fell from his chair when I told him he would have to be quick with the tests as I was due to fly to India the following week. Of course, there was no way he would recommend I fly, so I resigned myself to the fact that for the time being I was grounded.

I learned one of the reasons why Baba didn't want me to go to Kodai as soon as the group who did go came back. The weather was so bad and damp got into everything. Even when laundry was returned freshly ironed, it was still wringing wet, and the young healthy men in the group suffered from respiratory complaints. With my susceptibility to bronchitis I would have been in danger.

It has taken me a while finally to get the message that God loves us all and knows what is best for us. We can only see a small part of the picture of our lives and our goals are usually for short term advantages, whereas our loving Father/Mother sees the whole picture and if we stay in touch with our deep soul selves then we will be guided towards our greater good. At the time of my first Sai meeting at the Isle of Wight I did not know of these things, and, as I have already explained, I used my considerable organisational skills to try to join a group to India in 1991. It was all to no avail, and I had to accept that my long dreamed of trip to Mother India to visit the Ultimate Guru was not to take place until October, 1992.

CHAPTER FOURTEEN

*There are three types of behaviour among human beings: the Divine, the human and the animal. What we are witnessing is the growth of animality and decline of humanness. The reason for this trend is the limitless growth of desires and the steady disappearance of ideals (*assayaalu*). Selfishness is growing, selflessness is declining. Trickery is spreading, Integrity is vanishing, Attachment to the body is waxing, Love for the country is waning. The result is that the character of the people is getting degraded'*

- Sathya Sai Baba

'As I sit here waiting for a glimpse of my beloved and feel His all-encompassing love and compassion, I allow my eyes to wander through the maze of glorious colour. From the palest gold to the most vibrant orange, there is every hue, and I am filled with comfort, bliss and love.

Where am I sitting? Thoughts of exotic, rose filled gardens and some clandestine meeting may have passed through your mind, or you may, depending upon your inclination, think I am sitting on silk cushions under a mosaic Alhambran dome with a book of verse and a glass of wine until my Arab master can spare me a few precious perfumed filled moments of passion.

As sometimes happens in life, however, the truth is stranger than fiction. I am, in fact, sitting on a dirt floor on a very inadequate cushion, shoeless and squashed, with hardly room to breathe, between rows and rows of Indian and Western women, sticky and sweating under a hot Indian sun, waiting for a man claimed as an Avatar (God who takes human form): Bhagavan Sri Sathya Sai Baba.'

I WROTE THE ABOVE ON the front page OF a writer's folio notebook on 31st October, 1992. That is as far as I got with the book of my experiences that I had intended to write. I do not enjoy writing; I was emphatic as I handed in my last dissertation at University that it would be the last I'd write. My friends know me, and never expect more than a few lines of scribble very infrequently. It was a bit much to ask of myself in October, 1992, to spend my time writing, yet I had felt a prompting to share some of my spiritual experiences. This time, however, although I still don't like writing, I am more obedient to my inner voice which I know is the voice of God.

In fact, I had the idea for the title *God Lives in Stoke-on-Trent* in the spring of 1995, when I thought, 'Oh no, it looks as if I'm not going to get away with not writing of my experiences'. I managed to put off the evil hour, however, all year - I was extremely busy at the office and with the Workshops I had started to run in Stoke - at least that was my excuse.

I was *told* to take my writing material to India for my planned second trip in January, 1996, and I sat dutifully in darshan (like a blessing from the Pope) with hands held in prayerful position, prepared for a lovely relaxing meditation when I heard the inner voice say, 'Get on with your book.' I was shocked and quickly took out the folio note book and scribbled the title and opening paragraph. I stopped.

Why was I doing it? I don't want worldly fame and fortune. I have been along the path of material gains and, although I'm not a millionaire, I have always enjoyed abundance in my life. I am also becoming more and more reclusive; I certainly don't want fame.

I then had an internal conversation with Sai Baba. I spoke to Swami: 'You know I don't enjoy writing, but, to express my love for you, I will do it as *seva* (work dedicated to God), but you must really let me know in a physical sense that you want me to continue writing by blessing this book.'

Those who have been to Sai Baba's ashram at festival time will know how hard it is to be on the front row - this is usually reserved for VIP guests and college students, yet I was on the front row and although many people were vigorously thrusting various items out to him to bless he ignored all of them and just as he was passing me, simply holding my book and *japamala* (prayer beads) on my lap, he touched the book in blessing.

CHAPTER FIFTEEN

Avatars teach mankind lessons about how to realise God. Humanity needs Divine teachers to redeem it from its troubles. This is the purpose of Avatars, who come down to show mankind the ways of realising the Divine. You must recognise this truth. The Divine does not make the descent as an Avatar without a purpose. The purpose is to enable Nature to fulfil its role. To be born as human beings is a rare blessing. The Avatar instructs humanity how to redeem human existence.

- Sathya Sai Baba

THAT FIRST TRIP TO INDIA in October, 1992, had been quite an experience. One of our group has a photo of me kissing the ground as I touched Indian soil - just like the Pope! What a drama queen! It was done with all sincerity, however, because this was the end of my searching and a coming home to beloved India. Baba was at his residence in 'Whitefield', close to Bangalore, and my first darshan saw me sitting in great excitement about six feet away from where He would walk.

He came, and I saw for the first time the man who I knew was God in human form when I first read 'Transformation of the Heart'. He seemed to glide, not walk, and the vibrancy of His robe and His face is hard to describe. I was enthralled and watched attentively as He glided towards the section where I sat.

He stopped in front of where I was sitting and seemed to be looking for someone. It was me! He caught my eye and said, I clearly heard this in my head, 'Oh good, you're here.'

That was it! It was all I needed to send me into a state of bliss which lasted for the whole week we were at Whitefield. I was with what Victoria, a woman with a wicked sense of humour like mine, and I came to term 'the group from hell', and there were many bickerings and much unloving behaviour going on between the twenty or so women cooped up like pigeons in a cote. I was floating above it all. I even lay on a mattress crawling with bugs, normally a thing I would have been horrified at doing, and yet I was reluctant to rise, feeling that the bugs too were God's creatures and were not harming me.

Of course, because we live in a world of duality, there has to be an opposite, and the opposite to bliss is despair, and I certainly came to know this when I got to Prashanti Nilayam, otherwise known as the 'spiritual prison'.

I think the most distressing aspect of the ashram was the examples of man's inhumanity to man, demonstrated every day by the *seva dals*, the stewards who were the SS of the place. One day I was walking with the crowd of women from Darshan when a very old lady suddenly lurched at me and clung to my arm. She was very old, with crinkled, dark skin like parchment and only a few rotten teeth in her mouth. She was dressed in a rather old sari and she jabbered away at me in a language I thought may be Urdu, the dialect of the district. She could hardly walk, and I accompanied her very slowly so that she would not fall. I was in a bit of a dilemma because we had been asked not to give money to beggars - although I had ignored this and given to poor people outside the ashram. This old lady, however, was inside the ashram and in any case, I didn't want to offend her if she was poor but proud. I then hit on a perfect solution. I was on my way to the bake shop and I would offer to buy her whatever she wanted.

Suddenly I heard a commotion which broke my train of thoughts. I looked to my left in the direction of the noise and I was horrified by what I saw. A particularly cruel *seva dal* who was an Indian lady, but looked more like a male member of the German gestapo, was beating a young mother over the head, while another equally harsh *seva dal* was holding the young woman's baby which had been snatched from its mother's arms and which was now screaming with tiny arms outstretched. The mother was desperately trying to get her baby back, and clinging to her skirts and in a state of shock - a tiny toddler.

I couldn't believe my eyes. My instincts are such that without pausing to feel fear I rush in where I think help is needed. I have been known to attempt to stop two men fighting so I definitely was going to spring to this young mother's defence. The problem was that I was stuck with this old lady. She was still jabbering away at me as if she had not seen the commotion, and she leaned very heavily on my arm. I knew if I left her for only a second, she would not be able to stand and would surely crash to the ground. I desperately looked for someone to pass her over to, but everyone had moved further towards the area where the commotion was.

I couldn't believe that no-one was attempting to stop the horror we were watching, and I called out to anyone listening to stop them. By this time the *seva dals* were leading the mother, baby and child away and I slowly walked with the old lady, still leaning heavily on my arm, towards the bakery queue. Then she suddenly let go of my arm and disappeared into the crowd. I was still too shocked by what had happened to wonder how someone who had not been able to walk without my help had then let go and disappeared so quickly, and how, in fact, she had got to me in the first place.

It was two years later while I was attending a Phyllis Krystal workshop in London that I realised how strange the old lady's behaviour was. I was relating this tale to Phyllis as an example of one of the reasons why I would never go back to the inhumane ashram. 'You know who that was,' Phyllis said, and then it slowly dawned. Of course, I had heard of Baba appearing in times of stress, and often as a craggy old man or woman, and, of course, the reason he did this at this event was to stop my interfering, for I would surely have been thrown out of the ashram by the authorities and my group would then have had the scapegoat it needed to blame for the fact that we didn't get a much coveted private interview with Baba.

This incident confirmed what I had been trying to avoid thinking about, namely that there was more love and light in the worst dive than in this so called 'abode of peace'. I also questioned Baba.

I heard often of his sacrifice in coming out to give darshan twice a day, but I was not impressed with this. I could think of far more demanding jobs than 'swanning' around in a frock while hordes of handsome young men gazed adoringly up at Him.

After the *seva dal* incident I was very disappointed and went back to my camp bed in a concrete shed like an aeroplane hangar, and railed at the whole ashram and Sai organisation, particularly at this egocentric man whom everyone was convinced was God. God indeed! More like the Emperor with his non-existent clothes.

I didn't lose my faith in God, however. How could I deny my experiences of the all loving formless God I had seen during my near-death experience at my daughter's birth? But I did doubt the Sai Baba debacle. Then I read His words.

I had bought a couple of translations of His discourses, and I started to read what He actually says, and I could find nothing but pure Truth in his words. He spoke of love being the energy of the universe, and of the need for us to love each other and to recognise that we are part and parcel of God. He also said that God resides in everything and therefore everything is God, including us. I had already come to this truth, so here it was given to me in the words of Sai Baba. I was still glad, however, to leave the ashram and vowed I would never return.

I had been asked to give a talk about my Indian experiences to a group of truth seekers in Stoke, and I spoke to the organiser, a very dear friend, Lilian Elkin, and said I did not have good things to say about the ashram. She said perhaps I could talk about Findhorn instead. Now that was more like it. In fact, I talked about both I compared the two and you can guess which got the fewer votes.

It took a year for me to integrate my Indian experience, and what I came to understand was that just as the world has extremes of behaviour, then so does the ashram as a reflection of that world. I also now know that what was happening to me externally was a reflection of my internal state. The world is a mirror which does not judge, but simply reflects what we have locked inside our psyche.

I also realised from this whole ashram experience that we cannot judge God by the people who profess to worship Him. In every religion and spiritual belief system there are people who will distort the Truth, sometimes with deliberate intent, in order to control, as in the case of the Catholic Church when the Council of Constantinople in 400 AD left out the aspects of the scriptures that they felt gave away the Church's power, and sometimes with unconscious motivations simply because a lack of self-knowledge.

I have found, along with many others, that the search to find some meaning in life begins as a self search which then leads back to God The reason is that at our core, we are God. We are each made in His image. Only our negative ego thoughts and certain religious fundamentalists tell us that this is blasphemy.

I know that just as a liver is made up of individual cells, yet each is a liver cell and is part of the whole, then so too are we individual cells, yet one cell of humanity. I somehow felt this truth a long time before I began my self-search, when I used to work for Oxfam. I didn't understand why then, but I intuitively felt that we in the West could not simply close our eyes to the rest of the starving world, that in some way we were affected. That was over twenty-five years ago, and we now have much evidence for the inter connectedness of the whole planet. What happened in industry in Great Britain caused acid rain in The Black Forest; deforestation in Columbia affects the everglades in South America, etc. And the reason is simple. We are all part of the whole. One or two dead cells will not make a diseased kidney, but more than this will. The earth is one living organism, and what greater whole our earth is a part of, we can only gaze at the stars in wonderment and guess.

I know now that everything starts with the self. If each individual uncovers the layers of untruths about herself which she has collected over many lives, then she will find the golden nugget at the core which is her true nature - God.

CHAPTER SIXTEEN

Detachment, Faith, and Love - these are the pillar on which Peace rests. Of these, Faith is crucial. For, without it, Sadhana (spiritual practice) is an empty rite. Detachment alone can make Sadhana effective and Love leads quickly to God. Faith feeds the agony of separation from God; detachment canalises it along the path of God: Love lights the way. God will grant you what you need and deserve; there is no need to ask, no reason to grumble. Be content, be grateful whatever happens, whenever it happens. Nothing can happen against His Will.

- Sathya Sai Baba

I HAVE ALREADY SPOKEN of my numerous 'dark nights of the soul'. In January, 1995, true to form, I went into a deep depression, yet somehow this time, although it was still very painful, one part of me was able to stand back and witness what was happening. I knew that the process was growth promoting and that some creative thoughts would flower. This time I emerged with the words ringing in my head: 'JUST DO IT'.

I knew of a few things I had to 'just do'. One was to start a workshop based on Phyllis Krystal's work. The first of its kind in Stoke-on-Trent, and with added features from the many other workshops I had attended. The format had been given to me more than two years earlier while I was meditating one morning, and yet I had talked about doing it, but not actually put it into form. The other was to write a book, perhaps from research I wanted to do on the phenomenon of near-death experiences, the latter under the auspices of studying for a Master's Degree at Keele University.

There followed a frenetic period when I arranged for the local Stoke newspaper, the *Evening Sentinel,* to publish an article about the proposed workshop. With the help of my wonderful staff Denise, and Melanie, angel job sharing secretaries, and Rachael, our lovely young receptionist holding the fort, I quickly devised the fly sheets and application forms and the very first workshop of its kind took place in Stoke-on-Trent in March.

I also saw Helen Graham about the possibility of my undertaking near death experience research and she was very enthusiastic and supportive. In the meantime, however, I myself enrolled myself on a workshop run by Eileen Caddy, one of the co-founders of Findhorn, and called 'Inner Listening'. I had been keeping a journal for a number of years and writing when I felt the need; this was usually recording dreams which I could remember and which seemed significant, and any spiritual or emotional struggles I had, plus the occasional breakthroughs. Sometimes I would wake up in the morning or during meditation (which for me simply means lying still and emptying my mind) and a sentence or word would pop into my head. I would write these in my diary, yet, although one part of me knew that the words were not my usual style, I had doubts that they were from God. I think this was ego in action again, but in contrast to the usual boasting manner, this time it told me I wasn't worthy to receive God's words:

'Who do you think you are, Eileen Caddy?' I said to myself.

Whilst I was on Eileen's wonderful workshop, I experienced an unusual phenomenon. I was sitting in my favourite place, the nature sanctuary, which is a round igloo type building set in a beautiful garden and had lit a candle, as usual, and was enjoying the deep peace. I was sitting with my hands open and cupped on my knees when, as usually happens, I felt a burning sensation in my palms. What was unusual this time was that I felt a light pressure and then a sensation of moving balls of heat circling around my palms. I was intrigued. This had not happened before, and so the next morning, when I found Eileen sitting quietly before the day's lessons started, I told her about it, and asked her whether she had ever experienced this. She said she hadn't, and in reply to my questioning her as to what she thought this was, she said, 'Val, why don't you ask?' Simple, yet I hadn't thought to do this.

I went that evening to the sanctuary and sat with pad and pen by my side and waited. Again, the balls of moving heat held me enthralled and then I asked God what this was. I wrote down the words which came into my head and the next morning I timidly told Eileen what had happened. I also told her that I still had doubts about whether this was my ego or not, and she asked me to read the words to her. She sat on her chair, this beautiful, silver haired lady, and closed her eyes while I read my reply. When I finished she looked at me with such love and tenderness, and said, 'That is not your ego, my dear, that is God.'

Ever since this time I have regularly written down what I receive, sometimes in reply to a question but usually I leave the subject matter to God. The words pop into my head one at a time, so that I don't see the sense until I've finished, and the words flow so smoothly. There is never a crossing out as when my ego writes and is trying to find a suitable word.

I now know that each and every one of us is God. We are all made out of the same stuff as God. He made us this way and only because we wanted to experience the results of our own will, we have forgotten this. I love the old story of the meeting of the gods who sat on Mount Olympus to decide about the fate of man. They were considering where to hide the secret of life from human beings, and the god of thunder said, 'Hide it in the clouds. They won't find it there.' The god of the sea said, 'Hide it in the depths of the ocean. They'll never find it there.' This went on with various suggestions, until the last god came up with the solution: 'Hide it in their hearts. They will never think to look for it there.'

I know that the idea that we are all God will shock some people. It certainly shocked me when I was asked at a workshop to write down all the reasons why I thought I wasn't God. Me, God? What a preposterous idea, and the old Methodist early training made me feel decidedly uncomfortable so that I could not consider the notion even in the negative. God was somewhere up there, wasn't He, and hadn't I experienced Him as light but still out there and not in my own self? Yet my search to discover who I was and to dig down into the dark recesses of my psyche have brought me full circle. As we are made of God what else can we find when we peel away the layers of illusion? The search for Self has to lead to God, and we have discovered the secret hiding place of the ancient gods.

My particular path has led me to Bhagavan Shri Sathya Sai Baba, who is an Avatar. Hindu religion is the oldest recorded religion in the world, and the Vedas, the oldest scriptures, are the basis of all other religions. Baba himself has said that He has not come to change anyone's religion: He has only come to assist man to know who he is, which is The Divine *Atma, Atma* meaning essence. He says He wants the Muslim to be a better Muslim and the Christian to be a better Christian. This fits the notion I had when I was first on Helen Graham's workshop when I said that God was above all religions and that religion should be a way of finding God. I also could not believe what some religious groups claim, namely that the God of love I had experienced first-hand could possibly ignore three quarters of the world and just be supportive of a small group. Any loving mother or father knows that, even though we may be distressed with one of our children's behaviour, we still love that child as much as the others. How much more then, does God love us all? He loves the saints and the sinners alike. He loves those people who claim He does not exist and those who in ignorance mock Him. Each one of us is as dear to Him as the others, and no-one is held in more regard than anyone else. Exclusivity is not of God, who is all encompassing and inclusive.

I remember on my first trip to India I was lying on in my camp bed in the sheds.

The other members of the group had all left for better accommodation, and I was on my own and raging against Sai Baba's inhumane ashram when I worked out the following equation:-

$$God = Love$$
$$God = Spirituality$$
$$Love = Spirituality$$

I remember the look of exasperation on my partner's face when I rushed back to tell him that he was spiritual and not an atheist, as he claimed, because he was a loving man!

CHAPTER SEVENTEEN

Life is a pilgrimage, where man drags his feet along the rough and thorny road. With the Name of God on his lips, he will have no thirst; with the Form of God in his heart, he will feel no exhaustion. The company of the holy will inspire him to travel in hope and faith. The assurance that God is within call, that He is ever near, nor is He long in coming, will lend strength to his limbs and courage to his eye.

- Sathya Sai Baba

I AM SO GRATEFUL for the way in which my life has prepared me for the meeting at last with my own soul. Although I have not had an easy life, I can see that the lessons I have learned from the pain have been leading me back to my loving, God filled core. Fortunately for me, I have been on workshops with some of the world's leading metaphysical thinkers, and I also thank my solid Stoke-on-Trent background for helping to keep my feet firmly on the ground. I had already developed what William Bloom calls our 'bullshit antennae'. I could easily have developed into one of the spiritual 'fruit cakes' who, lovely as they are, cannot function in the physical world and turn a lot of people away from

God. Who wants to be like them? I also thank God that I was able to attend the workshops which for me have resulted in the greatest growth. An Elizabeth Kubler-Ross facilitator told me that Elizabeth has said that one of her intensive four-day workshops is worth two years of one-to-one psychotherapy. I see workshops as the way therapy is moving, as we enter the 21st Century. With good facilitators who have done a lot of their own work, yet who know that they still have lessons to learn, and are there simply to act as guides, an individual can progress more quickly in the search for health and peace of mind.

In the workshops I have held in Stoke I realise that I am simply the hostess who is throwing a party. Instead of the usual mix of males and females, I am there to allow self and Self, in other words egos and souls, to meet. All I have to do is act as interpreter when there is a difficulty in communication between the two.

I offer this book to God in the hope that someone may be encouraged to find the God residing in his/her heart. If I can do it, then absolutely anyone can. I humbly offer this writing to my Guru God, Bhagavan Shri Sathya Sai Baba, without whose love and guidance I would not have written it. I struggled to begin, as I do not want the ego trappings of wealth and fame, and could see no reason why I had to write it, but if just one person is inspired to begin the search, then the effort has been well worth it.

Perhaps now the title 'God Lives in Stoke-on-Trent' may be a little clearer. Because I am a part of God, as each one of you is too, and because I live in Stoke-on-Trent, then it figures that God really does live in Stoke-on-Trent. Simple!

Embodiments of Love! Your foremost aim today should be to recognise the power of love, God, dwells in everyone's heart as love incarnate. The goal of life is to recognise this truth and share your love with those around you.

Every human being should deem self-realisation as the main purpose of life and dedicate all his activities to the service of his fellow-beings, with constant remembrance of God as the indweller in all. This is the way to redeem one's life.

Develop Love,
Scatter Love,
Reap Love.

There is no religion higher than that.'

Baba

♥

AFTERWORD

In January 1997, I again went to India this time with the draft of this book neatly typed and copies of some of the 'writings'.

I sat in the sweltering heat for ten hours each day with the manuscripts in a plastic folder sticking to my back as I sat in my little chair inside and outside Sai Baba's temple. If I was anywhere near the front, I would remove them and hold them out to Him, but He never even glanced at me.

This went on for three weeks and, on the last evening before I was due to leave the following day, I wrote a letter in which I asked Him if He wanted me to revise and publish the work. I invited Him to take the letter if this was His wish and if He did not take it, I would know that He didn't want me to do anything with it. He did not take the letter.

I skipped back to the flat I was sharing with my friend Anne. I felt such relief that I didn't have to do anything more and felt so light-hearted as if the school holidays had begun. Maybe Swami simply wanted me to prove to him that I would do as He bid and write this account of my spiritual journey to do just that, and now the task was finished. Not so!

The following morning was my last darshan (blessing in the temple) before I left to journey to Rishikesh and I was so glad I could go without taking the books. However, I thought I may as well take them as I had done for the three previous weeks, so once again I found myself with a sticky plastic folder at my back.

In the ashram we queued to get into the mandir for Sai Baba's blessing and the person at the front of each line was invited to draw a number from a hat. I was in the line which drew seventeen so I would be a long distance from the front. However, I felt so blessed just to be in the ashram that I was not disappointed at this, and in any case I knew that I would get nearer to the front when Swami went into His interview room. This is the time when most of the devotees leave the temple to get refreshments.

I managed to move forward to row three and sat contentedly while Swami was in His private room with some of the important dignitaries who had come to see Him. Someone moved from the second row and I was able to shuffle into the space. Then something unusual happened. A lady in the coveted front row turned to me and said 'Would you like to sit in my space?' I didn't even know her. This prevented the usual squabble in the rare event of someone leaving the front row, as those in the second row try to take the precious space.

I sat here in bliss waiting for a glimpse of Swami. Then a remarkable event occurred. He left the temple before we had started bhajans, the devotional singing. He took the quickest route to his private quarters and those of us who were waiting stared at each other in confusion. What did this mean? Was He coming back? He had not done this in the previous three weeks or at any time that I knew of. In a few moments, however, He was back again, but instead of taking the short route back, He came along the line where I was sitting. With my heart pounding I quickly took the manuscripts from my folder and sat with them on my lap.

He walked towards the temple and away from me, but then He paused and turned towards me. I could hardly breathe. My friend Anne who was sitting behind me said that He said, 'You are leaving today?' How did he know this when there were five thousand people in the Ashram? I didn't hear this; I was too stunned because He was actually looking at ME. I held the book out and stammered 'Your book, Swami.' He gave a deep penetrating stare at the books and I knew that He was reading them, then He said 'Yes, do'. This was in answer to my letter, which I still held and which He made a deliberate point of removing from my shaking hand. In the letter I had asked Him if He wanted me to revise and publish the book and writings.

♥

THANK YOU
for reading
God Lives in Stoke on Trent.

If you enjoyed this book, please leave a review on the site where you bought it.

Reviews help other readers find books they may enjoy.

Pentalpha Publishing Edinburgh
pentalphapublishing.weebly.com

Bhagavan Shri Satya Sai Baba
Further details may be found at:
https://psg.sssihms.org.in/founder

ACKNOWLEDGEMENTS

I would to thank Mike Turner for reading the draft and spotting spelling mistakes; Nigel Simm for his reading of the draft and for putting it into computer format; and Barbara Scott Emmett who started it all by giving me a writer's portfolio and without whom it would not have come to be published.

After being told by Sai Baba to publish it has taken me over twenty years to do as I'm told.

Printed in Great Britain
by Amazon